The AI-Powered Professional

AI Productivity for Business Professionals
Without the Technical Overwhelm

Bruce Fleck, PhD

BJF Media Group

For information contact: https://brucefleck.com

BJF Media Group

ISBN-13: 978-1-7355798-5-6
First Edition: June 2026
10 9 8 7 6 5 4 3 2 1

Contents

Foreword

Transform from AI User to AI-Powered Professional (Without Losing Your Human Edge)

I've had the pleasure of working with Bruce Fleck for a few years now inside the Gen AI University community. And I'll say this without hesitation.

Bruce shows up. He doesn't just talk about using AI. He digs in. Experiments. Teaches. Shares what works and just as importantly, what doesn't.

Over time, he's become one of the most respected, consistent contributors in our world, and someone I continue to learn from every time he drops a new insight or framework.

But before we get into what Bruce has built here, let me zoom out and share why this matters so much to me... and why it should matter to you too.

Back in late 2020, I was looking for leverage. I was running a creative strategy business focused on eCommerce and Amazon listings.... work that was effective, but time-intensive.

My roommate at the time and one of my best friends, Austin Distel, was working at a Y Combinator backed startup that got early access to OpenAI and asked if I wanted to become a customer to try it out for myself, buying $100 in credits and becoming their first customer.

Of course I said yes. That tool would come to be known then as Conversion AI... then Jarvis... and now known as Jasper... almost 2 years before ChatGPT hit the scene.

These early days were the first time people like me could experiment with generative AI in a way that could actually be useful.

And when I saw what it could do, something clicked.

I realized that AI wasn't just here to help me write faster. It could reframe how I worked entirely.

I dove in. First came the Amazon listings. Then blog outlines. Then came the thought... if I can write a post this quickly, what about a book?

So naturally, I locked myself in a room for a weekend, cranked out a "minimum viable book," and published it on Amazon. That single move opened the door to new clients, new opportunities, and the insight that started it all: AI isn't just a tool to execute tasks. It's a thought partner.

Since then, I've built systems, communities, and frameworks around that core principle.

From the 7-Day Book Challenge, to the launch of The AI Author and now Gen AI University, to automating workflows and blueprint generators we've developed for real-world businesses, we've stayed committed to one thing:

Thinking with AI, not outsourcing thinking to AI.

And Bruce gets this at a fundamental level.

What makes his work stand out is not just the strategic thinking or the frameworks (though they're solid). It's that he never lost the human side of the process. His approach starts with empathy.

With context. With clarity of purpose.

This book isn't about replacing your workflow. It's about refining how you see it (and yourself) through the lens of AI.

Bruce walks you through what we call the AI-first mindset. Every project starts with the question, "How can AI help me think through this better?"

That shift is powerful. Because once you stop seeing AI as just a tool, and start treating it like a creative collaborator, everything changes.

But don't get it twisted. This is NOT about automating your brain.

AI is a mirror. It reflects what you feed it. If you give it junk, it multiplies junk. But if you lead with clarity, strategy, and purpose, it'll help you unlock what's been sitting in your blindspots all along.

That's why the professionals who truly thrive with this tech aren't the ones who rely on templates or chase the next trend. They're the ones who know how to set context, ask better questions, and stay anchored in human judgment while moving faster, deeper, and more creatively than ever before.

Bruce has mapped out exactly how to do that in this book.

He's lived it. He's taught it. He's helped others apply it across industries. And now, he's laid it all out for you so you can integrate these tools without losing yourself in the process.

If you want a no-nonsense guide to becoming an AI-powered professional? One rooted in real practice, real results, and real integrity? You're in the right place.

Read this with curiosity. Apply it with intention. And enjoy the ride.

—Darby Rollins
Founder, GenAIUniversity.com

Chapter 1

The AI Imperative

Why This Matters More Than You Think

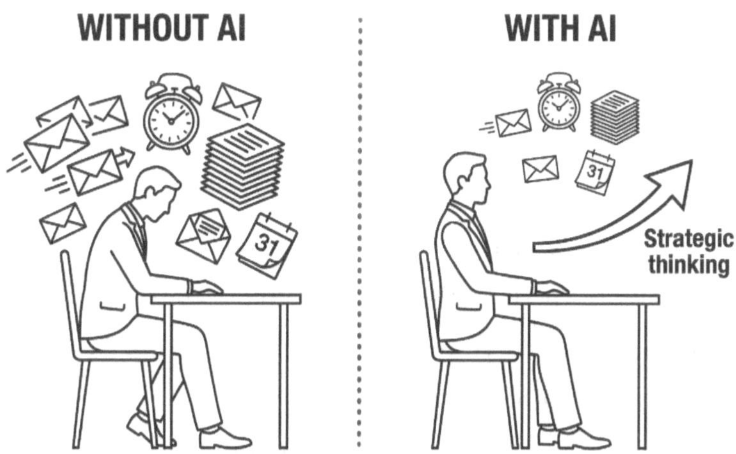

Same role. Same experience.

Picture two professionals. Same role. Same company. Same experience level.

One of them spends Monday morning manually drafting six client emails, researching competitor updates by clicking through a dozen websites, and formatting a presentation slide by slide. She's competent. She's thorough. And by lunch, she's exhausted, with half her to-do list still waiting.

The other one drafts those six emails in her tone and style in twenty minutes with AI, gets a competitive landscape summary in ten, and generates a presentation framework in fifteen. By lunch, she's moved on to the strategic work, the planning, the relationship building, the creative problem-solving that no tool can replicate.

Both professionals are good at their jobs. But only one of them is keeping pace with where professional work is heading.

The gap between these two isn't talent or intelligence. It's awareness, an awareness that something fundamental has shifted and that the shift is accelerating.

The Numbers Don't Lie

Here's where things get real.

Seventy-five percent of knowledge workers are now using AI at work. Not experimenting. Not "thinking about it." Using it. According to research from Microsoft and LinkedIn, AI adoption has more than doubled in just the past year.

AI users report saving more than an hour per day. That's five hours a week. Over two hundred hours a year. Think about what you'd do with two hundred extra hours of professional capacity.

And here's the number that should stop you cold:

71% of leaders say they'd prefer to hire a less experienced candidate with AI skills over a more experienced candidate without them.

Read that again.

Your years of experience, the hard-won expertise you've built over your career, is being weighed against a skill set that most professionals haven't bothered to develop. That's not a threat to dismiss. That's an opportunity to seize.

This moment is different from previous technology waves. When email replaced memos, there was a learning curve but the adjustment was gradual. When social media hit, businesses adapted over years. AI is moving faster than both.

Consider the pace. ChatGPT launched in November 2022. Within two months it had a hundred million users, making it the fastest-growing consumer application in history. By early 2023, every major tech company had released competing AI tools. By 2024, AI was embedded in Microsoft Office, Google Workspace, and most major business platforms. This isn't a slow-moving trend you can evaluate from the sidelines. The train has left the station.

But here's the encouraging part. The fundamentals of working with AI effectively haven't changed nearly as fast as the tools themselves. The principles you'll learn in this book, how to communicate clearly with AI, how to provide context, how to iterate, work today, worked a year ago, and will work a year from now. Building foundational skills now positions you to absorb every advancement that follows.

The Training Gap (And Your Opportunity)

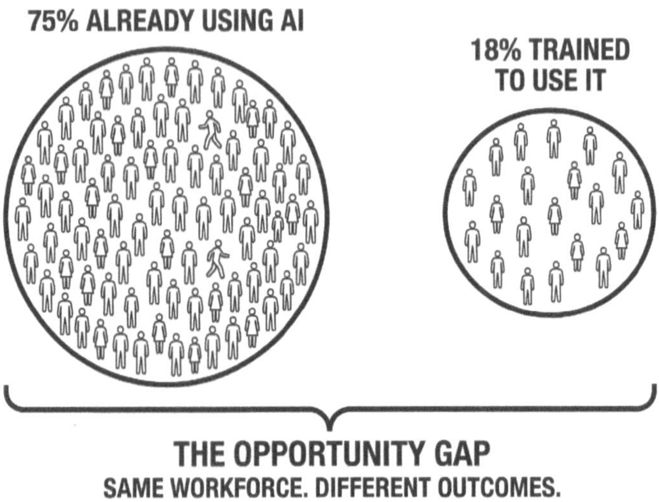

But here's what makes this moment so strange:

> **82% of employees receive no formal AI training from their employers.**

Think about that disconnect. Three-quarters of knowledge workers are using AI, yet more than four out of five have never been taught how. They're figuring it out on their own, by trial and error, by watching YouTube videos, by asking a colleague who seems to know what they're doing.

This is where the real story is. You're not behind because you lack some innate ability. You're not behind because you're "not technical enough." You're behind because nobody has taught you.

That's not a criticism. It's actually good news. Because the gap between where you are and where the AI-enabled professionals are isn't as wide as it feels. It's a knowledge gap, not a talent gap. And knowledge gaps can be closed quickly when you have the right framework.

The opportunity sitting right in front of you is enormous. Companies are still figuring out their AI training programs. Professionals who invest in their own development now gain a head start that compounds over time.

Your Hidden Advantage

Here's something that might surprise you. Your professional experience is actually your biggest advantage with AI. Not a disadvantage. An advantage.

The professionals who struggle most with AI aren't the non-technical ones. They're the ones who don't have deep domain knowledge, who don't understand the problems worth solving, who can't evaluate whether AI's output actually makes sense in context.

You know your industry. You know your clients. You know what good work looks like in your field. You understand the nuances that a generic AI output misses. That judgment, that experience, that contextual understanding, that's exactly what AI needs from you to produce exceptional results.

Let me give you a real example.

In April of 2023, I ran a class called the 10-10-10 AI-Powered Lead Generation Program for a group of 38 coaches and professionals, including life coaches, health coaches, spiritual coaches, and business coaches. One of the participants was Carol, a life and mindset coach.

Carol is a senior which is not what most people picture when they imagine someone embracing AI. She has basic computer skills and would be the first to tell you she isn't particularly tech-savvy. She isn't a natural early adopter. But she came in with something that matters far more than technical confidence. She was willing to learn, and curious enough to experiment.

And Carol had something even more valuable than technical skills. She understood her audience. She knew what her clients struggled with, what language they used, what kept them up at night. And when she learned how to communicate that knowledge to AI, how to give it the context it needed, something remarkable happened.

Carol didn't just learn to use AI. She started *teaching* it. Within months, she created and launched a course called **"AI for Seniors"**, teaching basic AI access, logging in, everyday use cases, going beyond simple Q&A.

Think about that transformation for a moment. A woman who describes herself as "not technical," who came into the class cautious and unsure, walked out and built an entirely new coaching program around AI education. She didn't just cross the gap between AI-resistant and AI-enabled. She became someone who helps others cross it.

And the ripple effect matters too. Every senior Carol teaches becomes another person who can use AI in their daily life. One person's breakthrough enables dozens more. That's the kind of compound impact we're talking about.

Carol's story also dismantles one of the most persistent myths about AI. AI adoption no longer follows generational lines where younger people adopt easily and older people struggle to keep up. Carol is proof that AI has no age limits. It doesn't work that way.

Anyone with basic computer skills can learn to use AI effectively. What it requires isn't youth or technical background. It's the desire to learn, the curiosity to experiment, and the persistence to work through challenges. Those qualities have nothing to do with age, and everything to do with mindset.

Carol's story isn't unusual. It's the pattern. The professionals who succeed with AI aren't the ones with computer science degrees. They're the ones who bring domain expertise, clear communication skills, and a willingness to start.

You already have the first two. This book gives you the framework for the third.

What's Actually Possible

I don't want to just tell you that AI saves time. I want to show you what that actually looks like.

After I developed my approach, combining AI with proven expert frameworks (which I'll teach you throughout this book), I started tracking specific time savings on real projects:

- **A complete opt-in funnel**, including landing pages, thank-you pages, and email sequences, went from eight hours of work to one hour.
- **An effective sales page** went from a week of writing to four hours.
- **Complete marketing content packages**, including landing pages, email sequences, and social media posts, took a fraction of their traditional production time.

And here's the part that surprised me most, the quality didn't go down. It went *up*. Because instead of spending my energy on the mechanical work of writing and formatting, I could focus on the strategic thinking, the positioning, the messaging, the audience understanding that actually determines whether something works.

The compound effect is what makes this transformative. When you reclaim hours from routine tasks, those hours don't just disappear. They become available for the high-value work that advances your career, grows your business, and makes your contribution genuinely irreplaceable.

What to Expect

Learning any new skill takes time before it saves time, and AI is no different. In the beginning, tasks will often take a little longer than your usual approach. That's completely normal. Don't let early slowness convince you that AI isn't working. You'll never reach the time savings AI can deliver if you skip the learning phase.

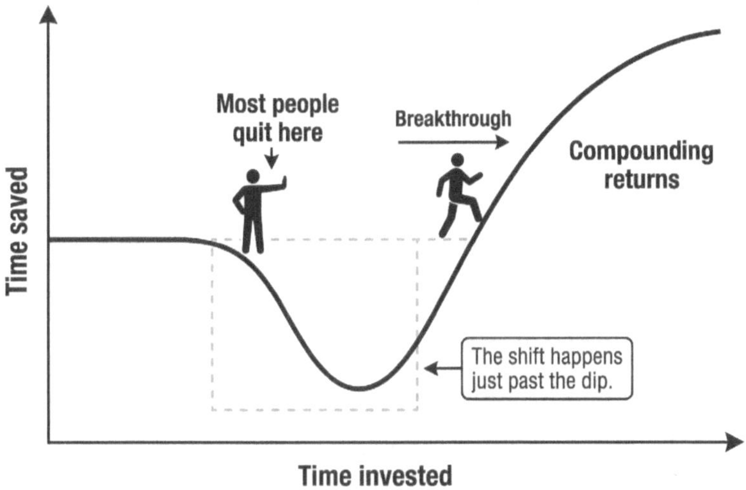

The numbers I shared above didn't happen on day one. My first attempt to use AI for a sales page took almost as long as writing it from scratch, because I spent more time editing bad output than I would have spent writing good copy myself. Sound familiar?

The shift happened when I stopped treating AI as a magic button and started treating it as a professional collaborator that needed clear direction. As my skills built and I developed prompts I could reuse, things started moving faster, then significantly faster. That's the pattern every professional goes through.

The difference between "AI wastes my time" and "AI saves me eight hours on a funnel" was a set of skills and principles, the exact ones you'll learn in the chapters ahead. The time savings are real.

But they're the result of learning how to work with AI effectively, not just having access to the tool.

Your Starting Point

You don't need to become an AI expert overnight. You don't need to master every tool. You don't even need to be particularly good at technology.

What you need is to start. And starting is simpler than you think.

This week, try these three things:

1. **Notice how often AI comes up** in your professional world, in meetings, in articles, in conversations with colleagues. Just observe. You'll be surprised how pervasive it's become.

2. **List three tasks** where you'd love to have an assistant. Not complex strategic work, just the routine stuff that eats your time. Emails you write every week. Reports you format every month. Research you do before every meeting.

3. **Identify one colleague** who seems to be succeeding with AI. Not to compare yourself, but to notice that they're not fundamentally different from you. They just started.

Common mistakes to avoid right now:

- **Waiting for perfect training before starting.** There's no such thing. The best training happens while doing real work.
- **Comparing yourself to technical early adopters.** They have different skills, not better ones. Your domain expertise is the advantage they wish they had.
- **Assuming AI is "all or nothing."** You don't need to transform your entire workflow overnight. Start with one task. Then another. Then another.
- **Your quick win for today:** Open ChatGPT, Claude, or whatever AI tool you have access to, and ask it to summarize an article you need to read. That's it. One task. See what happens.

Instead of typing "Summarize this article", use this prompt instead:

"Review the attached article (or article URL). Extract the Situation, Problem, Key Insight/Big Idea, Important Points written as topic and brief description, and Action Steps."

Get the Free Companion Course

Reading about AI builds knowledge. Doing it builds skill. The free **AI-Powered Professional Foundations Lab** is designed to turn the principles in this book into hands-on experience, one chapter at a time.

The course has eight lessons, one for each chapter. Each lesson takes about fifteen minutes and includes a hands-on prompt exercise that produces a real, useful output, not a practice exercise you discard after finishing. Over the eight lessons you'll build an AI opportunity audit for your own workflow, a polished deliverable created using all seven prompting principles, a personalized strategy for overcoming the obstacles that stop most professionals, and a 30-day integration roadmap. By the end, you'll have eight concrete outputs you can use and refer back to.

This companion course is free. It's the fastest way to close the gap between understanding these principles and actually using them. By taking action while the ideas are fresh, you'll learn faster, get better results sooner, and build the momentum that carries you forward.

Get free access at: https://aibizpro.link/aipp-course

Understanding why AI matters is step one. But what actually *is* AI, and how do you use it without getting lost in technical jargon? Let's clear that up next.

Chapter 2

Work Smarter

The Promise That Didn't Deliver

It was a summer evening in 2022, and I was staring at my screen in disbelief.

Four thousand words. The AI had just generated four thousand words in about thirty seconds. I leaned back in my chair and had one thought. *This would have taken me eight hours.*

I was working on my coaching program, called The Crisis Cure that teaches a five-step framework for navigating a mid-life crisis. I wanted to write a blog post called "Why Professionals Are Likely to Experience a Life Crisis." So, I fired up Word Hero, an early AI writing tool I'd purchased as a lifetime deal, typed in my topic, and hit generate.

Four thousand words appeared on my screen like magic.

Then I started reading.

The first paragraph wandered off-topic. The second made claims I couldn't verify. By the third, I realized the AI had essentially written a generic article that could have appeared on any self-help website on the internet. And worst of all, it didn't sound like me at all. I couldn't in good conscious post this with my name on it.

Here's what was even more disappointing. When I tried to edit and reshape those four thousand words into something I could actually use, *the editing took more time than writing from scratch would have.*

I sat back and stared at the blinking cursor. That rush of excitement had changed into something else entirely. Disillusionment.

This is not a magic wand, I told myself. *It's going to take some skill and knowledge to make these new AI tools useful.*

If you've had a moment like this where you tried AI, got disappointing results, and wondered if you were "just not technical enough". I want you to know you're not alone. And you're not wrong that AI should be able to help you. The problem isn't the technology. The problem isn't you, either.

The problem is that nobody taught you how to actually communicate with these tools.

The Technology Hype Curve

There's a pattern that plays out every time a major new technology arrives. It's so predictable that researchers have mapped it, and it's called the Technology Hype Cycle. What it describes is exactly what you and I have been living through with AI.

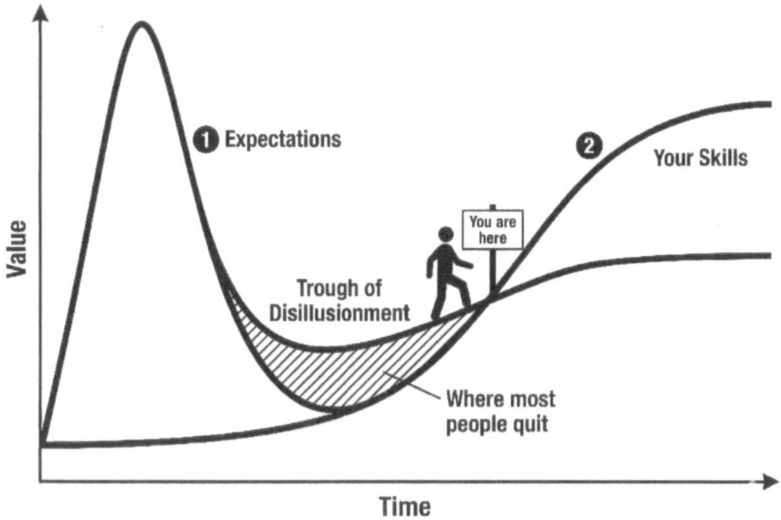

Here's how it works.

A breakthrough appears. Early results look spectacular. The buzz builds fast. Tech media writes breathless headlines. Gurus start talking about it in courses, at conferences, on social media. Their presentations are loaded with claims about what this technology will soon be able to do.

Notice those last words. *Will soon be able to do.*

That gap between what the technology actually does today and what enthusiasts promise it will eventually do is where the trouble starts. Expectations race ahead of reality. And when real people try it themselves, they crash into that gap.

With AI there's a second layer that makes things especially tricky. The hype cycle tracks the technology itself. What it doesn't show is the *skills gap*, the distance between what you'd need to know to use AI effectively and what most people actually know the first time they open a chat window.

The technology curve shoots upward, then crashes into what researchers call the Trough of Disillusionment before slowly climbing toward real productive value. The skills curve builds gradually, through practice and experimentation, through learning from people who've already worked it out. The space between those two lines is where most people give up.

So who pushes through?

Not the most technically skilled. The people who make it through that trough are usually ordinary people who decided the technology mattered enough to figure out. A practitioner buried in paperwork. A coach who needed more time with clients. Someone who saw what was possible and decided they weren't going to be left behind.

What they brought wasn't technical expertise. It was three things. A genuine commitment to learn because it connected to something that actually mattered to their career or their goals. A curiosity about how things worked and how they didn't, and a willingness to experiment without expecting immediate results. And enough persistence to push through the early awkward stage before things started clicking.

Those three qualities matter far more than tech background.

The gap between the hype you heard and the results you got isn't a sign that AI doesn't work. It's a sign that you needed a map for closing the skills gap.

That's what this book provides.

This Story Is Older Than You Think

Here's what might surprise you. My frustration with AI didn't start in 2022. It started five years earlier.

In 2017, I sat at my computer staring at a questionnaire that stretched down the screen. A software program called Wordbotic promised I could write a book in a single weekend. Having already spent roughly a hundred hours on a traditionally written book, that promise was incredibly appealing.

I filled in the blanks. I answered every question. I followed the system exactly.

The output? A rigid, fill-in-the-blank short ebook. No voice. No flow. You could practically see the template seams. It was immediately recognizable as machine-generated.

That same year, I tried Jim Edwards' 3-Hour Kindle Book Wizard. Same hopes. Same result.

I'm telling you this because I want you to understand something important. I wasn't a late adopter who suddenly discovered AI when everyone else did. I was an *early* adopter who kept searching, kept trying, kept believing that technology could help professionals like us work smarter. Even when every tool I tried fell short.

The technology just wasn't there yet.

But I kept looking. And eventually, the technology caught up.

Then in November 2022, ChatGPT 3.5 arrived. And within the first conversation, I knew something had fundamentally shifted.

This wasn't an incremental improvement. The AI could hold a natural conversation. It could refine its output when I pushed back. It could take a complex idea and break it down intelligently. For the first time, I was *collaborating* with a thinking partner.

The challenges were still there. It hallucinated at times making up facts and answering confidently. It gave overly wordy responses that needed trimming. A learning curve to figure out how to communicate effectively with this new kind of tool.

But beneath those challenges? Transformative potential.

Within months, through systematic experimentation and connecting with other AI enthusiasts, I developed an approach that combined AI with proven expert frameworks. My success rate climbed. Soon 60% of outputs needed only minor editing. Then 70%. Then 80%.

The gap between "AI is a gimmick" and "AI is a game-changer" turned out to be a skill gap. And that skill gap is exactly what this book closes.

AI Education Mismatch

Here's what nobody tells you about AI, and it's not what you think.

You're not bad at technology. You're not "too old" to learn new tools. You're not missing some gene that makes AI adoption easy for everyone except you. What you're experiencing is a fundamental mismatch between how AI is typically taught and how professionals actually need to learn.

Most AI education falls into one of two traps.

Either it's too technical or too superficial. Either you're drowning in terms like "neural networks" and "machine learning algorithms" that have nothing to do with writing better emails or analyzing spreadsheets faster. Or you're getting generic tips like "just experiment!" without showing you how to get useful results.

But here's the thing. Using AI effectively isn't about understanding how the technology works inside. You don't need to know how your car's engine functions to be an excellent driver. What you need is a clear framework for knowing when to use which gear, how to navigate different road conditions, and what to do when something unexpected happens.

That framework doesn't exist in most AI training because the people creating it come from technical backgrounds. They assume you want to understand the machinery. But you're not trying to become an AI engineer. You're trying to stop drowning in busy work so you can focus on the strategic thinking that actually moves your career forward.

Here's what I discovered about those professionals who seem to have figured out AI. They didn't take a course on machine learning. They didn't read a four-hundred-page technical manual. What they found, often through the same frustrating trial and error you've been through, was that AI works best when you treat it like a capable but literal-minded collaborator. The quality of what you get out depends entirely on how clearly you communicate what you need going in.

This is why my first attempts felt so disappointing. I asked AI a vague question and got a vague answer. I expected magic and got mediocrity. That wasn't a limitation of the technology. It was an expectations versus skills gap. And that gap can be closed.

Chasing Tools versus Learning Principles

There's another piece to this puzzle. Most professionals try to learn AI by jumping from tool to tool, chasing every new application that promises to revolutionize their work. They're overwhelmed by options and underwhelmed by results.

What they're missing is a systematic progression. What they and you need is a roadmap on how to build skills in a logical sequence, starting with simple time-savers and gradually expanding to more sophisticated applications.

The professionals thriving with AI today aren't necessarily the most technically skilled. They're the ones who found a structured approach that matched how they actually work and learn. They started small, built confidence through quick wins, and progressively expanded their capabilities.

That structured approach is exactly what this book provides.

Your Tuesday Morning, Reimagined

Imagine waking up on a Tuesday morning with a completely different relationship to your work.

Your inbox still has emails. That hasn't changed. But instead of spending ninety minutes crafting individual responses, you collaborate with AI to draft replies in fifteen minutes, adding your personal touch to the ones that need it. That quarterly report? You finished the first draft yesterday afternoon. AI helped you analyze the data, organize the insights, and structure the narrative. What used to consume a full day of focused work took three hours.

Picture yourself walking into your team meeting actually prepared. You've already reviewed the agenda, and you've identified the three points where your input matters most. When a colleague asks for help on their presentation, you don't feel that familiar knot of resentment. It's just one more thing on your overloaded plate. But now it's manageable. Instead, you spend twenty minutes collaborating with AI to generate solid talking points, add your refinements, and send them off. The whole thing takes half an hour and delivers real value.

You're not working harder or longer. You're redirecting your energy from the tasks that drain you to the work that energizes you.

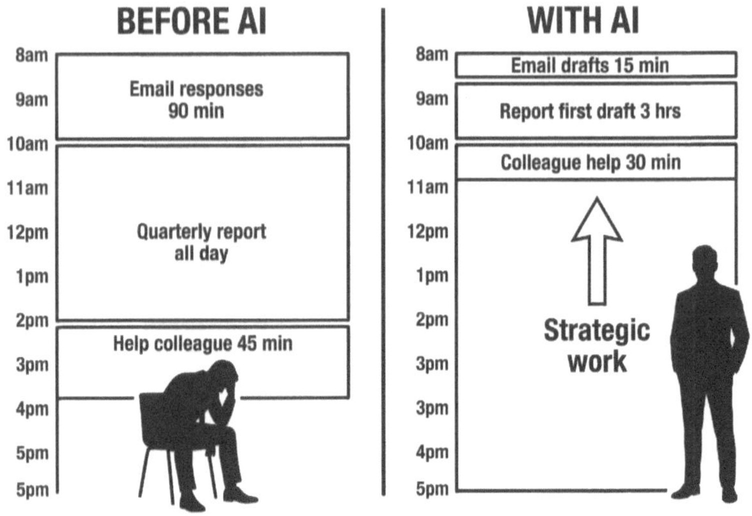

Think about what becomes possible when you reclaim ten hours every week from routine tasks. Maybe you finally have time to develop that strategic initiative you've been putting off. Maybe you take on a stretch project that positions you for the promotion you've been working toward. Maybe you simply leave work at a reasonable hour and have dinner with your family without checking email every ten minutes.

The professionals who've made this transition describe it the same way. *I got my actual job back.* Not a different job, but the one they signed up for before it got buried under administrative overhead and communication management.

Six months from now, you could be the person your colleagues turn to for AI advice. Not because you became a technical expert, but because you figured out how to make AI work for your specific professional context. You'll know which tasks to accelerate, which outputs to amplify, and when AI can help you perform at levels that previously required years more experience.

The gap between AI-enabled professionals and those who haven't started is widening every day. Every task you complete manually while a colleague leverages AI puts you one step behind. But here's the encouraging truth. Closing that gap doesn't require a technical background, a massive time investment, or a dramatic lifestyle change. It requires a framework, some focused practice, and the willingness to work through initial awkwardness until the new approach becomes natural.

That transformation is closer than you think.

Your Skill Development Roadmap

This book introduces the **A4 AI Integration Framework**, a systematic approach I developed from my own journey and from watching how successful professionals actually learn and apply AI to their work.

The framework has four progressive stages:

1. **Accelerate:** Do what you already do, but in a fraction of the time. Before AI, routine tasks like drafting emails, preparing summaries, or writing first drafts consumed hours you didn't have. Now you have a capable assistant that handles the heavy lifting while you focus on the parts that actually need your expertise. This is where most professionals start, and for most, the time savings show up within the first week.

2. **Amplify:** Multiply your impact by elevating the depth and quality of your work. Before AI, most professionals only had time to make things good enough. Now you have a thinking partner that helps you make them really good. Reports become more thorough, proposals more polished, and that same stronger work can reach further too, becoming a presentation, a social post, or a talking point for your next meeting.

3. **Augment:** Access capabilities that used to require years of additional experience or a team of specialists. Before AI, expert-level analysis, sophisticated frameworks, and higher-level strategy were largely out of reach for solo practitioners. Now you can apply those methodologies through AI, producing deliverables that would have required expertise you simply hadn't had time to build. Your professional judgment stays at the center, and AI extends how far it reaches.

4. **Automate:** Build systems that do the work with minimal supervision. Before AI, creating a reliable, repeatable process for high-quality outputs meant building detailed templates and spending significant time in quality control. Now you can design workflows where work that used to take hours or a whole team can be done in minutes, with AI handling the execution and you stepping in only where your judgment matters most. This is where the real

leverage lives, freeing you to focus entirely on the work that moves things forward.

This book is your foundation. It gives you the understanding, the communication skills, and the framework you need to begin. Each subsequent book in the series goes deep into one A4 stage.

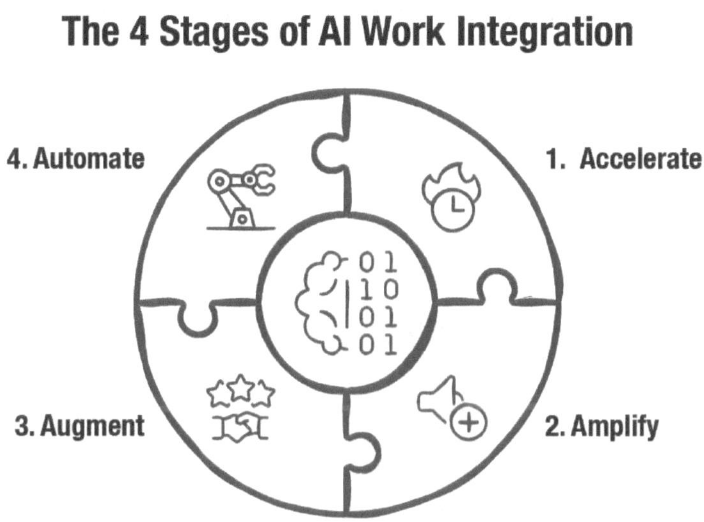

Here's what you'll find in the chapters ahead:

Chapter 3: Demystifying AI, just enough technical understanding to work effectively, without the jargon overwhelm

Chapter 4: The A4 Framework, your complete roadmap from beginner to AI-powered professional

Chapter 5: Overcoming the Hurdles, the obstacles that stop most people, and specific strategies to push through each one

Chapter 6: The Prompting Foundation, the communication skills that turn generic AI outputs into exactly what you need

Chapter 7: Your Quick Wins, proven first steps that build confidence and create immediate value

Chapter 8: Your AI-Powered Future, your personalized path forward and what comes next in the series

Each chapter includes practical exercises you can complete in under ten minutes. You don't need to set aside special learning time. You'll build AI skills while doing your actual work.

The path from where you are to where you want to be isn't as long as it seems. Most professionals start seeing meaningful time savings within their first week of applying these principles.

Let's begin.

Take the Next Step

Now jump over to **AI-Powered Professional Foundations Lab** to work on a lesson that pairs directly with this chapter. In that lesson, you'll do an AI Opportunity Audit of your own work. You'll list the tasks you do every week, use AI to score each one for AI-readiness, and rank them by where you'd save the most time. You walk away with a prioritized list of your best starting points, not a generic recommendation but one built around your actual job. It takes about fifteen minutes and gives you a clear answer to the question most people get stuck on. Where do I even begin?

Access the lesson at https://aibizpro.link/aipp-ch-2

Chapter 3

Demystifying AI

The Conversation You've Been Faking

You're in a meeting. Someone mentions "large language models" and how they're going to "transform our workflow." A colleague nods enthusiastically and says something about "generative AI versus predictive AI." Your boss asks if anyone has looked into "fine-tuning models for our use case."

You nod along. You make a note. You look interested.

Inside, you have one thought. *I have no idea what any of that means. And I'm terrified someone is going to ask me a direct question.*

If that's you, take a breath. You don't need to understand any of those terms to use AI effectively. In fact, most of the people throwing around that jargon don't fully understand it either. They've just gotten comfortable with the vocabulary.

What you need is just enough understanding to work confidently. Not enough to build AI systems. Not enough to pass a computer science exam. Just enough to know what you're working with, what it can do, and, just as importantly, what it can't.

That's exactly what this chapter gives you.

What AI Actually Is (And the Simplest Way to Think About It)

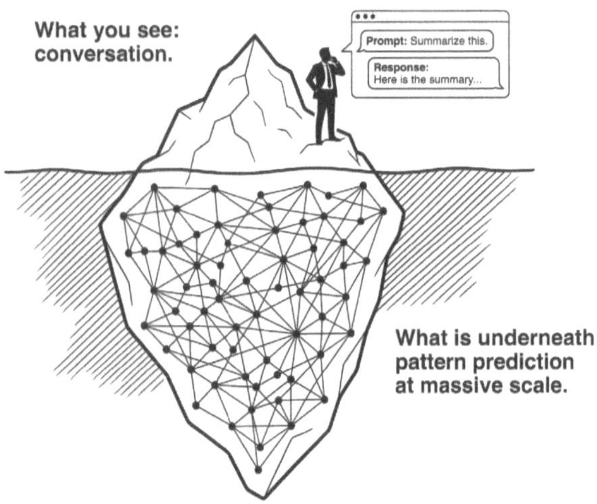

Let me give you the most useful definition of generative AI I've ever found. I've used this with every student, every client, every coaching group I've worked with. It's the one that consistently turns on the light bulb.

Generative AI is a word prediction machine trained on the general internet.

That's it. That's the core of what tools like ChatGPT, Claude, and Gemini do.

When you type a prompt, the AI isn't "thinking" the way you and I think. It's predicting, at massive scale and remarkable speed, what words should come next based on patterns it learned from billions of pages of text on the internet.

Now, here's why that simple definition changes everything about how you use AI.

It explains why generic prompts get generic results. If the AI is trained on the general internet and you give it a vague request, it's going to pull from the most common, average patterns it learned. That's why "write me a blog post about leadership" gets you something that sounds like every other leadership article you've ever read. The AI is predicting the most *likely* words. The most likely words about leadership are the generic ones.

It explains why specificity transforms your results. When you give AI a role, a goal, specific context, clear instructions, and constraints, you're narrowing down what patterns it predicts from. Instead of drawing from everything the internet says about leadership, it's predicting words based on the specific scenario you described. The output gets dramatically better.

And it explains why your domain expertise is so valuable. The internet doesn't know your specific client. It doesn't know your company's culture. It doesn't know the nuances of your industry niche. But *you* do. And when you feed that knowledge into AI through well-crafted prompts, you get outputs the internet alone could never produce.

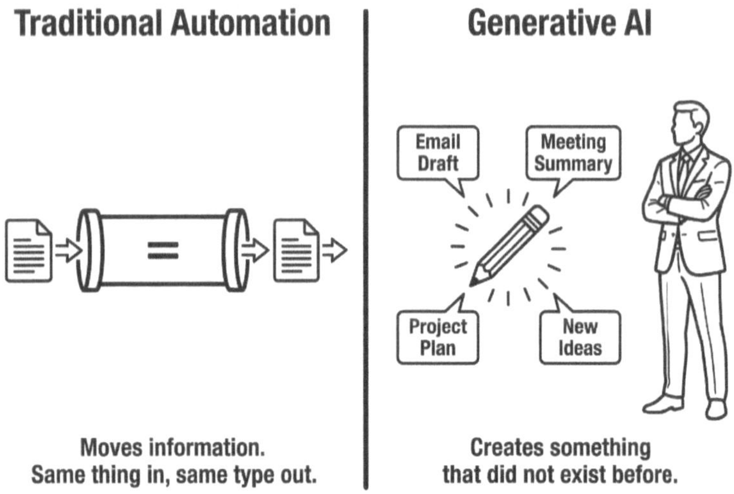

Before generative AI, I worked with tools like Zapier, automation software that could move information between applications. Copy an API key here, paste it there, and suddenly your payment processor talks to your WordPress site, which updates your database. Useful stuff.

But those tools *moved* information. They couldn't *generate* new ideas. They couldn't create content, synthesize perspectives, or help you think through a problem. They operated within strict parameters. If this happens, then do that.

Generative AI is fundamentally different. It creates. It synthesizes. It reasons (in its way). Understanding this distinction matters because it sets the right expectations. You're not working with a fancy search engine or a souped-up calculator. You're working with something that generates new text based on the patterns it's learned. Your job is to guide those patterns toward what you actually need.

The Tool Landscape (Without the Overwhelm)

Right now, you're probably aware of at least a few AI tools. ChatGPT. Claude. Gemini. Maybe you've heard of Midjourney for images or Copilot from Microsoft. New tools seem to launch every week.

The most useful thing you can do right now is to **ignore most of them.**

The single biggest mistake I see professionals make is trying to keep up with every new AI tool announcement. They download five apps, sign up for three platforms, and end up mastering none of them.

Here's a better approach:

For text-based AI (which is where 90% of your professional value sits):
Pick one. ChatGPT, Claude, or Gemini. Any of them will work. They each have strengths.

ChatGPT has the largest user community and the most tutorials available

Claude tends to produce more natural, nuanced writing

Gemini integrates well with Google's ecosystem

Pick whichever one you have easiest access to. Start there. Master it. You can always add others later.

For everything else: Not yet. Images, video, audio, coding. These are all real AI capabilities, but they're not where you start.

Master text-based AI first. The principles you learn here transfer to every other type.

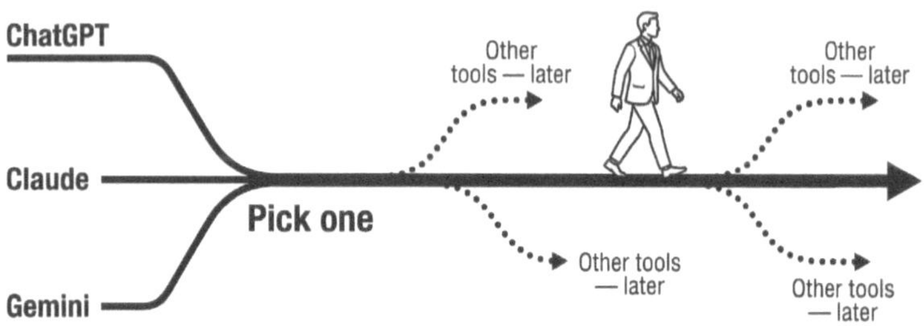

One strong foundation beats three shallow ones.

I learned this lesson the hard way. Between 2017 and 2022, I tried tool after tool, including Wordbotic, Word Hero, Jasper, and more. Each one promised to be the answer. Each one had a different interface, different strengths, different limitations. I spent more time learning tools than I spent actually producing useful work.

The tools from 2017 aren't the tools of today. Not even close. If someone tells you "I tried AI and it didn't work," the most important question is what they tried and when. The tools evolving from 2022 to today represents one of the fastest capability leaps in technology history. What produced rigid, template-like output three years ago now generates nuanced, contextually aware content that often surpasses what most professionals can produce from scratch.

What AI Can and Cannot Do

This is where realistic expectations save you from the disappointment cycle that stops most people.

AI CAN:

- **Process and synthesize large amounts of information.** Give it a long document and ask for a summary. Give it data and ask for patterns. Give it a complex situation and ask for analysis. This is where AI shines. It processes information faster than any human, without getting tired or distracted.

- **Draft content in multiple formats.** Emails, reports, presentations, social media posts, proposals. AI can generate first drafts at remarkable speed. Not final drafts. First drafts. That distinction matters.

- **Brainstorm and generate ideas.** Need ten angles for a marketing campaign? Twenty questions for a client interview? Five ways to restructure your team meeting? AI is an inexhaustible brainstorming partner that never gets tired or self-conscious.

- **Research and gather information.** Need background on a competitor? Want to understand a new regulation?

Looking for best practices in an unfamiliar area? AI can give you a solid starting point faster than traditional research.

- **Analyze patterns and provide different perspectives.** AI can help you see your work from angles you hadn't considered, your customer's perspective, your competitor's perspective, a different industry's approach to the same problem.

AI CANNOT:

- **Make final decisions for you.** It can inform decisions. It can present options. It can analyze trade-offs. But the judgment call is always yours. This isn't a limitation. It's a feature. Your judgment is what makes AI output valuable instead of generic.

- **Replace your expertise.** AI can help a good marketer work faster. It can't turn someone who doesn't understand marketing into a marketer. Your professional knowledge is the lens through which AI output becomes meaningful.

- **Guarantee accuracy.** This is critical. AI can be confidently, convincingly wrong. It can cite statistics that don't exist. It can attribute quotes to the wrong people. It can make factual errors while sounding completely authoritative. Always verify important facts, numbers, names, and claims.

- **Understand your specific context without being told.** AI doesn't know your company, your clients, your industry norms, or your personal preferences unless you tell it. The more context you provide, the better the output. No context = generic results.

The professionals who get the most from AI are the ones who understand this balance. They use AI's strengths (speed, processing power, tireless ideation) while compensating for its weaknesses (accuracy risks, lack of context, inability to make judgment calls). They treat it as a powerful collaborator, not a replacement for their own expertise.

✓ AI Can	✗ AI Cannot
Draft and refine content	Verify facts reliably
Synthesize research quickly	Replace your judgment
Generate options and variations	Know your specific context
Analyze patterns in data	Guarantee accuracy
Adapt tone and style on request	Think strategically for you

The professionals who get the most from AI understand this balance.

Your First Real Interaction

Here's the thing about learning AI. You can't learn it by reading about it. You learn it by using it. So let's do that right now.

Action Step 1: Open your AI tool of choice.

If you don't have one yet, go to chat.openai.com and create a free account. It takes two minutes. If you already have access to Claude, Gemini, or any other tool, use that. It doesn't matter which one.

Action Step 2: Ask it to explain something from your field.

Type something like "Explain [concept from your profession] in simple terms that a new employee would understand."

Replace the concept with something you know well. If you're in marketing, maybe "explain content marketing." If you're in healthcare, maybe "explain patient-centered care." If you're in finance, maybe "explain cash flow management."

Notice what happens. The explanation will be decent, maybe even good. But it probably won't be exactly how *you* would explain it to a new employee. It'll be missing your examples, your analogies, your way of framing things.

That gap between what AI produces and what you would produce? That's your professional value. And in the next chapter, you're going to learn how to close that gap, how to communicate with AI so that its output sounds like you, addresses your specific situation, and delivers exactly what you need.

Action Step 3: Ask a follow-up.

Based on whatever AI generated, type this follow-up. "What's missing from this explanation that someone in [your industry] would need to know?"

Watch what happens. The AI will often surface useful additions. Some of them you already know. Some might be new. That's the beginning of a productive conversation, not a one-shot query, but a dialogue.

Common mistakes at this stage:

- **Trying to learn everything about AI before using it.** You'll learn faster by doing than by studying. Start now.
- **Getting distracted by every new tool announcement.** Pick one. Use it. Master it. Add others only when you've outgrown the first.
- **Expecting AI to be right 100% of the time.** It won't be. That's normal. Build verification into your workflow and you'll be fine.

Quick win:

Ask AI to give you three questions you should ask in your next meeting. You might be surprised at how useful the suggestions are, and how much time it saves compared to preparing those questions from scratch.

Now you understand what AI is and what it can do. The next step is knowing how to use it systematically. Chapter 4 gives you the roadmap for that, a clear progression from first experiments to full professional integration. And in Chapter 6, you'll learn the communication skills that turn that roadmap into real results.

Take the Next Step

The **AI-Powered Professional Foundations Lab** has a lesson that pairs directly with this chapter. In that lesson, you'll put AI's knowledge to the test in your own field. You'll ask it to brief a newcomer on a topic you know deeply, then evaluate the output yourself, marking what it got right, what was too surface-level, and what was flat wrong.

What you walk away with is a domain expertise gap analysis, a clear picture of exactly where AI is strong and where your professional knowledge is irreplaceable. It's also the moment most professionals stop seeing AI as competition and start seeing it as a collaborator.

Access the lesson at https://aibizpro.link/aipp-ch-3

Chapter 4

The A4 AI Integration Framework

When Random Experimentation Hits a Wall

You've been using AI for a few weeks now. Some tasks go well. Others don't. You're saving time on email drafts but struggling with longer documents. You got a great brainstorm session last Tuesday but a useless one on Thursday.

There's no pattern to what works and what doesn't. No progression. No sense of building toward something bigger.

This is where most professionals plateau. They've learned the basics, they see the potential, but without a framework for *how* to progress, they bounce between experiments without direction. Some days AI feels like a superpower. Other days it feels like a gimmick.

Here's what I discovered after years of this exact cycle. The breakthrough didn't come from finding a better tool. It came from finding a better *approach* to using any tool.

The Shift That Changed Everything

Same person. Completely different relationship with AI.

For the longest time, I treated AI as a task tool. I'd bring it a specific job, draft this email, summarize this document, brainstorm these ideas, and it would perform. Sometimes well. Sometimes not.

It was like having a brilliant assistant but only asking them to make copies and file papers.

Then the shift happened. I stopped asking **"How can I use AI for this task?"** and started asking **"How can AI help me think about and approach this entire project?"**

AI went from being a tool I used sporadically to a collaborator I engaged with systematically. Not just for execution, but for planning. Not just for speed, but for quality. Not just for individual tasks, but for complete workflows.

That shift, from task tool to strategic collaborator, is what the A4 Framework captures. It gives you a progression from basic usage to full integration, with clear stages so you always know where you are and what comes next.

The A4 AI Integration Framework

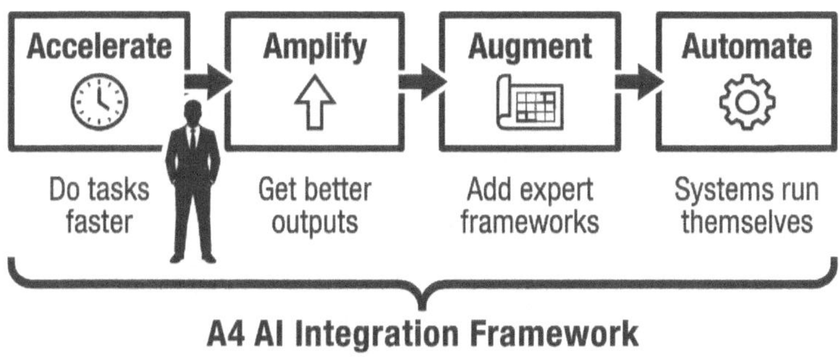

Each stage builds on the one before. You do not skip steps.

The framework has four progressive stages. Each builds on the previous. You don't skip stages. You advance through them as your skills and confidence grow.

Stage 1: ACCELERATE

Core question: *"How can I do what I already do, faster?"*

This is where you start. Acceleration means taking tasks you're already good at, tasks that are part of your regular workflow, and using AI to complete them in a fraction of the time.

What Acceleration looks like:

- Drafting emails in minutes instead of half an hour
- Summarizing long documents in seconds instead of an hour
- Generating meeting notes from your rough bullet points
- Creating first drafts of reports using data you provide
- Brainstorming twenty ideas in five minutes instead of staring at a blank page

The key characteristic: Your workflow stays basically the same. You're still doing the same work, making the same decisions, producing the same types of output. AI just makes it faster.

When you're ready for Acceleration: You have tasks you're good at that take too much time. You've been doing them manually and you know exactly what the end result should look like.

This is the lowest-risk, highest-confidence starting point. You already know what good looks like, so you can immediately evaluate whether AI's output meets your standards.

Stage 2: AMPLIFY

Core question: *"How can I multiply my impact without multiplying my effort?"*

Once you're moving fast, the next question becomes how to get *more* from the same amount of work. And "more" means two things.

First, it means higher quality and greater depth. A client report that used to run two or three pages can now become a one-page executive summary plus ten pages of in-depth analysis.

AI makes it practical to gather more data, conduct deeper research, and produce more comprehensive work than you could in the same amount of time before. The quality goes up. The depth increases. This is the work you always wanted to produce if only you'd had more time.

Second, it means greater reach. That same high-quality report can become a presentation, a set of social media posts, or an email series with minimal additional effort. One piece of strong work serves multiple audiences in multiple formats.

What Amplification looks like:

- A client report becomes a one-page executive summary plus detailed supporting analysis
- One analysis serves five different audiences with five different framings
- One research session feeds into three different projects
- One set of insights becomes a presentation, a LinkedIn post, and a team memo

The key characteristic: Same input, higher quality output, and more of it. You're not working harder. You're getting dramatically more value from the same effort. This is the stage where you really begin to see the power of what AI can do.

When you're ready for Amplification: You've mastered Acceleration and you're producing quality work quickly. Now you want that work to be better and go further.

Stage 3: AUGMENT

Expert-level work. Without the years of training.

Core question: *"How can I do things beyond my current skill level?"*

This is where things get genuinely exciting.

Augmentation means using AI to perform tasks that would normally require expertise you don't have, or would take years to develop. Not by pretending to be an expert, but by leveraging proven frameworks through AI.

What Augmentation looks like:

- Applying data analysis frameworks without being a data scientist

- Using marketing strategy frameworks you haven't studied
- Conducting financial modeling without a finance background
- Implementing project management methodologies for the first time

The biggest shift in my own journey came when I started combining AI with **proven expert frameworks.** Not asking AI to generate content from scratch. Using AI to *implement* established business and marketing strategies.

The results jumped dramatically. Outputs went from 60-70% usable to 80-90% final quality with minimal editing. The AI wasn't just following generic instructions anymore. It was implementing sophisticated strategies with remarkable precision.

The blueprint metaphor works here. Expert frameworks are like professional architectural blueprints. Without them, AI is building freehand, sometimes beautiful, sometimes unstable. With them, AI builds with precision because the structure eliminates randomness.

When you're ready for Augmentation: You've mastered Acceleration and Amplification. You're comfortable with AI as a tool. Now you're ready to expand what's possible.

Stage 4: AUTOMATE

Core question: *"How can I build systems that work without my constant attention?"*

Automation is the final stage, building repeatable workflows that run with minimal human intervention.

What Automation looks like:

- Recurring reports that generate themselves from updated data
- Customer communication sequences that adapt based on responses
- Data processing workflows that flag only what needs your attention

- Content calendars that populate based on your strategic themes

The key characteristic: Human oversight remains essential. You design the system, set the parameters, and review the output. But the execution happens without you sitting in front of a screen.

When you're ready for Automation: You have repeatable processes that follow predictable patterns. You've already Accelerated, Amplified, and Augmented. Now you're building systems from those capabilities.

The Progressive Path

Here's why the stages matter in sequence.

1. **Accelerate first.** You learn how AI works by using it on familiar tasks where you can immediately evaluate quality. This builds confidence.

2. **Amplify second.** You learn to think about AI strategically, not just "do this task" but "extract maximum value from this work." This builds capability.

3. **Augment third.** You learn to combine AI with structured frameworks, expanding what you can accomplish. This builds range.

4. **Automate fourth.** You learn to design systems, not just complete tasks. This builds leverage.

Each stage prepares you for the next. Trying to automate before you can accelerate is like trying to run a marathon before you can jog around the block. Not impossible, just unnecessarily frustrating.

This book covers the foundation, giving you the understanding, the prompting skills, and the framework overview you need to begin. Each subsequent book in the series goes deep into one stage.

Book 2: Accelerate, Master speed and efficiency

Book 3: Amplify, Multiply your impact

Book 4: Augment, Expand your capabilities

Book 5: Automate, Build self-running systems

The Framework in Real Life

IIn April 2023, I launched the 10-10-10 AI-Powered Lead Generation Program, ten weeks, ten hours per week, building a system to generate ten leads per week for online coaches.

The class was moderately successful. Looking back, I tried to cover too much too quickly. I was essentially trying to take coaches through multiple A4 stages before they'd mastered the first one.

But the class succeeded in one crucial area. It got every participant using AI on a daily or weekly basis. The coaches who stuck with the structured progression, start with acceleration, build from there, saw real results. The ones who tried to jump to automation before they could write an effective prompt? They struggled.

That experience helped me envision the A4 Framework. The sequence matters. The progression matters. You can be ambitious about where you're going, but you start where you are.

Here's a more specific example of what the progression looks like for one professional.

Imagine a marketing director named Sarah. She starts at **Accelerate**, using AI to draft her weekly email newsletter in twenty minutes instead of two hours. She's doing the same work, just faster. After a few weeks, she's comfortable and confident.

Then she moves to **Amplify**. She starts by bringing in examples from her best past newsletters and using them as a quality benchmark, so every new newsletter meets that standard. The quality goes up. It's not just faster. It's better. And once that stronger newsletter exists, it easily becomes a LinkedIn post, three social media updates, and a talking point for the company all-hands meeting. Better work, broader reach, same research.

Next, **Augment**: Sarah uses an expert competitive analysis framework with AI to produce quarterly market intelligence reports, something that previously required hiring an outside consultant. She doesn't have a market research degree, but the framework plus AI plus her industry knowledge produces excellent results.

Finally, **Automate**: Sarah builds a workflow where competitive mentions and industry news are automatically collected, summarized, and categorized, landing in her inbox as a weekly brief that requires ten minutes of review instead of three hours of manual research.

That's the A4 journey. From faster email to an automated intelligence system. But it happened step by step, each stage building capability and confidence for the next.

Mapping Your Opportunities

Here's an exercise that makes the A4 Framework immediately practical.

Think about five tasks you do regularly. For each one, ask:

1. **Could AI help me do this faster?** (Accelerate)
   Writing emails, summarizing documents, creating outlines, brainstorming

2. **Could the output from this task be improved in quality and serve multiple purposes?** (Amplify)
   Could a client report also become content? Could research feed multiple projects?

3. **Am I limited by skills I don't currently have?** (Augment)
   Could an expert framework + AI help me do this at a higher level?

4. **Does this task happen on a regular, predictable pattern?** (Automate)
   Weekly reports? Monthly updates? Recurring client communications?

Most professionals find that their biggest immediate opportunities are in Acceleration, and that's exactly where to start.

Your action steps:

1. **Map five of your regular tasks to the A4 stages.** Where do your biggest opportunities sit? Most will start in Accelerate. That's normal and right.

2. **Identify one Acceleration candidate for this week.** A specific task you know well, that takes too long, where you can immediately evaluate AI's output quality.

3. **Note one task in each other stage for future development.** You're not working on these yet. Just flagging them. Awareness of the progression is valuable even before you reach those stages.

Common mistakes:

- **Trying to automate before you can accelerate.** Walk before you run. Master the basics and the advanced becomes natural.

- **Skipping stages because they seem "too basic."** Acceleration isn't basic. It's foundational. Every subsequent stage depends on it.

- **Expecting to master all four stages immediately.** This is a progression measured in weeks and months, not hours.

Quick win:

Take one email or document you need to write this week. Open your AI tool and try a simple request. You'll build your full prompting foundation in Chapter 6. For now, just start. Time yourself. Compare it to how long that task normally takes.

You have the framework now. You understand the progression. You know where to start and where this leads.

But here's the truth. Knowing all of this doesn't guarantee you'll follow through. There are obstacles that stop most professionals cold, real, predictable hurdles that derail the best intentions.

The good news? They're all solvable. Let's tackle them head-on.

Take the Next Step

Here's where the A4 Framework stops being a concept and becomes your personal roadmap. Head over to the **AI-Powered Professional Foundations Lab** and work through the Chapter 4 lesson while everything is fresh. You'll take the highest-priority task from your own work and run it through all four lenses, not just to classify it, but to sketch out what each stage would actually look like for that specific task in your real job.

What you build is called an A4 Progression Map. A concrete picture of how your most important work could be accelerated, amplified, augmented, and eventually automated. It's the moment the framework stops being something you read about and starts being a plan you're actually following.

Access the lesson at https://aibizpro.link/aipp-ch-4

Chapter 5

Overcoming the Hurdles

The Professional Who Stopped

You've read the first four chapters of this book. You understand why AI matters. You know what it is and what it can do. You have the A4 Framework as your roadmap.

And there's a very real chance that none of it will matter.

Not because the information isn't good. It is. Not because you're not capable. You are. But because there are five predictable obstacles that stop most professionals from ever turning knowledge into action, and if you don't see them coming, they'll stop you too.

I know this because I hit every single one of them myself. And I've watched the same pattern play out in coaching classes, workshops, and one-on-one sessions with professionals across every industry.

Most people quit. You don't have to be most people.

Hurdle 1: "I Don't Know Where to Start"

Too many options. Too many tools. Too many possible applications. The sheer breadth of what AI can do creates a strange paralysis. You can see the potential, but you can't figure out where to put your first foot down.

I remember this feeling vividly.

When I started with Jasper, one of the early AI writing tools, it operated on a word-based credit system. Every word the AI generated cost credits. Every experiment burned through your allocation.

That credit system created a form of paralysis I didn't expect. I'd hover over the keyboard with one thought circling. *What if I write the wrong prompt? What if the output is useless? I'll have wasted credits for nothing.*

I was standing at the edge of the pool, not sure how deep the water was. So instead of diving in, I dabbled. Simple prompts. Low-risk experiments. Never committing enough to see real results.

The resolution? A structured class that *forced* me to pick a real project and commit. No more casual experimentation. No more tiptoeing around the edges. Pick a project with actual stakes and use AI to complete it.

The solution to "I don't know where to start": Start with one Acceleration task from Chapter 4. Not the biggest task on your plate. Not the most important one. Just a familiar task that takes too much time, an email you write regularly, a document you update monthly, a summary you create after every meeting.

Pick one. Do it with AI. Evaluate the result.

That's it. That's the start.

Hurdle 2: "I Don't Have Time to Learn"

This one is almost universal. Your plate is already full. Your calendar is packed. Learning a new technology feels like adding another project to an already impossible workload.

But here's what I want you to hear: **AI isn't a separate thing to learn. It's a tool you learn while doing your existing work.**

You don't need to block out a weekend for an AI bootcamp. You don't need to complete a certification course. You need fifteen minutes and a real task.

When I hit this hurdle, what broke through was investing not just in a tool, but in a *community*. I joined Darby Rollins' community, GenAI University, a course and network of professionals all learning together.

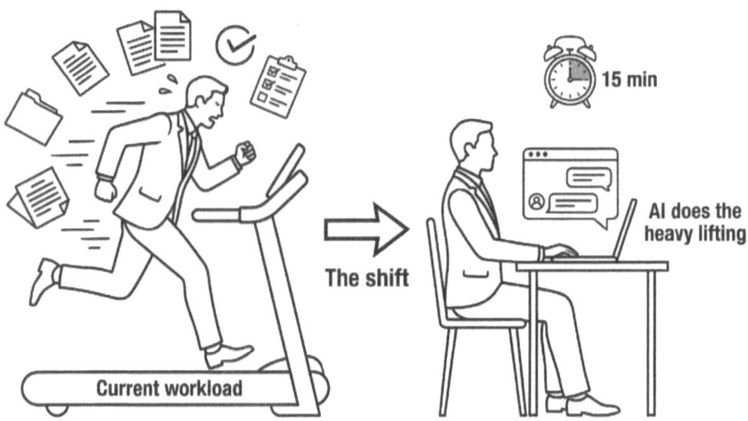

Learn by doing your existing work with AI. Not by studying separately.

Here's what I discovered. *"Technology was changing fast and new tools were coming out every day. Connecting with a community of professionals helped me avoid overwhelm, stay up-to-date, and continue developing skills."*

In a field that evolves as fast as AI, trying to learn alone is like trying to drink from a fire hose. You need people who are a step ahead pointing you toward what actually matters and away from what's just noise.

The solution to "I don't have time":

1. **Learn while working.** Don't set aside "AI learning time." Use AI on a real task. The learning happens automatically.

2. **Start with 15-minute experiments.** One task. One prompt. One evaluation. Fifteen minutes.

3. **Celebrate small wins and save what works.** When a prompt produces a good output, save it. Store your best prompts in a Word doc, Google doc, or any accessible location so you can reference and reuse them in the future. Skills compound faster when you build on what's already working.

The professionals who "don't have time to learn AI" are spending hours every week doing things AI could handle in minutes. The math isn't complicated.

Hurdle 3: "I'm Not Technical Enough"

This is the hurdle I hear most often. And it's the one that's most completely wrong.

The concern usually comes from exposure to technical AI discussions like machine learning, neural networks, training data, and fine-tuning. That stuff sounds intimidating. And if you needed to understand it to use AI, you'd be right to worry.

But you don't.

Building AI is engineering. Using AI is communication.

You don't need to understand how a car's engine works to be an excellent driver.

You need to know how to turn the key, use the pedals, follow the rules of the road, and get where you're going. The engine is somebody else's job.

AI is the same. The engineering behind large language models is somebody else's job. Your job is to communicate clearly with the tool, evaluate what it produces, and apply your professional judgment. Those are skills you already have.

Carol proves this. She wasn't technical. Not remotely. But she went from cautious AI student to teaching "AI for Seniors," making AI accessible to people even further from the technical world than she was.

She didn't need to understand neural networks. She needed domain expertise, clear communication skills, and a willingness to practice.

The solution to "I'm not technical enough":

Stop conflating "using AI" with "building AI." They're completely different activities requiring completely different skills. Using AI is a communication skill. You communicate professionally every day. You already have what you need.

Hurdle 4: "I Tried It and Got Bad Results"

One bad result is not a verdict. It is feedback.

This one's tricky because the experience is real. You tried AI. The output was disappointing. And the natural conclusion is that this doesn't work for me.

I've been there. More than once.

My journey looked like this. Word Hero in 2022 left me with four thousand words that were useless. Jasper produced decent templates but they were rigid and expensive. ChatGPT gave me confidently wrong answers that wasted more time than they saved.

Then I watched the same pattern repeat in my 10-10-10 class. Coach after coach hit the same wall:

1. Try AI
2. Get generic or unhelpful results
3. Conclude "it's not for me" (or "I'm not technical enough")
4. Stop

The universal pattern. And it has a universal cause. **The specifics gap.**

Generic inputs produce generic outputs. If you type "write me a blog post about wellness," you'll get the same article that would show up on any generic wellness website. Not because AI is bad. Because you gave it nothing specific to work with.

This isn't a technology problem. It's a communication problem. Chapter 6 gives you the solution. The 7 Prompting Principles.

If your early experiences with AI were disappointing, there's a very good chance the issue was in the prompt, not in the tool. Go back. Apply the principles. Try again. The difference will be dramatic.

The solution to "I tried it and got bad results":

1. **Revisit with better prompts.** Once you've worked through Chapter 6, apply the 7 Principles to the same task that disappointed you before. Compare the results.

2. **Break big tasks into smaller pieces.** Instead of "write my marketing plan," try "help me identify three key messages for my target audience." Smaller, more focused requests produce better outputs.

3. **Use the conversation, not just the first response.** The first output is a draft. Refine it. Give feedback. Iterate.

Hurdle 5: "There Are Too Many Tools and Constant Changes"

You cannot master every tool. Pick one. Go deep.

Every week there's a new AI tool, a new feature release, a new "this changes everything" announcement. If you feel like you can't possibly keep up, you're right. You can't. Nobody can. And nobody needs to.

This is FOMO at industrial scale, and it's designed to make you feel behind.

Here's the antidote. **Master principles that transfer, not tools that change.**

The 7 Prompting Principles in Chapter 6 work in ChatGPT. They work in Claude. They work in Gemini. They'll work in whatever tool launches next month or next year. Because they're based on how to communicate effectively with AI, and that doesn't change when the interface does.

Use two or three tools deeply. Let the rest go. When something genuinely revolutionary appears, you'll hear about it from your professional network. You won't miss it.

Think problem-first, not tool-first. Don't start with "what can this new tool do?" Start with "what problem am I trying to solve?" Then find the tool that solves it. Most of the time, the tools you already have will be sufficient.

The solution to "too many tools and constant changes":

1. **Pick one primary AI tool and master it.** Use it for 90% of your needs. You can always add others later.

2. **Focus on principles over platform features.** Everything in this book transfers across tools.

3. **Filter ruthlessly.** New tool announcement? Ask, "Does this solve a problem I actually have?" If no, ignore it.

The Mindset Shift That Makes It All Work

I want to share something that reframed my entire relationship with AI, something that came from a moment of genuine frustration.

It was during an early adopters class for business innovators. I'd enrolled, committed to a real project, and was struggling. My first "successful" prompt produced a wall of text that looked impressive until I tried to use it, a rambling mess that required more editing than writing from scratch.

I was frustrated. Discouraged. Wondering if I'd fundamentally misunderstood how AI worked.

Then the realization hit, *"This was the worst it would ever be."*

Every day forward, two things would happen. My skills would improve through practice. And the AI models themselves would get better through development.

I was standing at the bottom of a learning curve that only went up. The only direction was forward.

That reframing changed everything. It turned early struggles from evidence of failure into evidence that I was at the starting line. It made every awkward prompt attempt feel like practice instead of proof that I couldn't do this.

Whatever frustration you're feeling right now, whatever hurdle is loudest in your mind, remember that you're experiencing the worst version of your AI skills you'll ever have. Every day you practice, you get better. Every month, the tools get better too.

The dual compounding, your skills improving *and* the technology improving, means the gap between effort and results shrinks constantly. What feels hard today will feel natural in weeks.

Your Strategy for This Week

Don't try to solve all five hurdles at once. That's its own form of overwhelm.

Step 1: Identify your primary hurdle. Which of the five resonates most? That's the one to focus on.

Step 2: Apply the specific solution for that hurdle this week. One solution. One week. One focused effort.

Step 3: Notice when the hurdle voice appears, and do one small AI task anyway. The voice will say "you don't have time" or "this won't work" or "you're not technical enough." Acknowledge it. Then open your AI tool and spend fifteen minutes on one real task.

Common Mistakes:

- **Trying to solve all hurdles simultaneously.** Focus creates progress. Pick one.

- **Giving up after one bad experience.** One bad prompt isn't a verdict on AI or on your ability. It's a data point. Adjust and try again.

- **Comparing your starting point to someone else's**

current success. They started where you are. They just started earlier.

Quick Win:

When your primary hurdle voice speaks up this week, and it will, name it out loud. "That's the 'not technical enough' hurdle." Then do one small AI task anyway. The voice gets quieter every time you prove it wrong.

You know the hurdles now. You know they're psychological, not technical. And you know they're all conquerable.

What you need next is the skill to close the specifics gap. Not more reasons to believe AI can work. The practical principles that turn vague requests into useful output. That's what Chapter 6 delivers.

Take the Next Step

You've identified your hurdles. Now let's actually do something about them. In the **AI-Powered Professional Foundations Lab** lesson for this chapter, you'll use AI itself as a coaching partner to work through your primary hurdle. You tell it which one hit closest to home, and it helps you build a personalized strategy for moving past it.

You walk away with a specific reframe, three actions you can take that week to start proving the old belief wrong, and something to come back to the next time that hurdle shows up. It's one of the most direct uses of AI in the entire course, and honestly one of the most useful outputs you'll create.

Access the lesson at https://aibizpro.link/aipp-ch-5

Chapter 6

The Prompting Foundation

Same Question, Completely Different Answer

Let me show you something that changed how I think about AI.

Here's Prompt A:

> *"Help me with a project summary."*

And here's Prompt B:

> *"You are a senior project manager writing for a non-technical executive audience. I need a one-page summary of our Q3 website redesign project. The project was completed on time, 5% under budget, and in-*

creased mobile conversion by 23%. Highlight the business impact, not the technical details. Use confident, direct language. Structure it as: key achievement, business impact, next steps."

Same task. Same AI tool. Wildly different results.

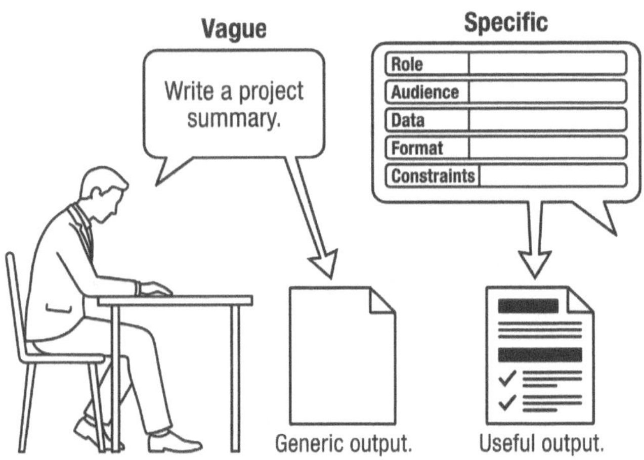

Same task. Same tool. The input made all the difference.

Prompt A gets you a generic template with placeholder text that reads like it was pulled from a project management textbook. Prompt B gets you a polished summary your CEO could actually read, one that took thirty seconds to generate and maybe two minutes to refine.

The difference isn't the AI. The difference is what you give the AI.

This chapter teaches you the communication skills that transform every interaction you have with AI. Not tricks. Not hacks.

Principles that work across any platform, any tool, any task, and that keep working as AI evolves.

Principle 1: You're the Expert, Not the Machine

This is the foundation everything else builds on, so let me be direct: **AI doesn't know what good looks like in your world. You do.**

When I first started working with AI, I did what most people do. I treated it like a magic box. Type in a request, hope for the best. The results were mediocre, and I assumed the technology was the problem.

But while most people in the AI space were busy selling pre-written prompt libraries, collections of templates you could copy and paste, I noticed something troubling. Those template collections were platform-dependent and inflexible. They worked like the fill-in-the-blank tools I'd been burned by before. Useful for narrow applications. Limiting for anything that required real judgment.

That realization led me to a fundamentally different approach. Instead of collecting prompts, I started studying the *principles* that made prompts effective across any platform. Not "use this exact prompt for LinkedIn posts." Instead: "Here's why this prompt works, and how to apply that understanding to anything you need."

It was like the difference between having a recipe for chicken parmesan and actually understanding how to cook. Master the techniques, and you can tackle any recipe.

The most important technique? Remembering that *you* are the expert. Your judgment determines quality. AI amplifies your expertise. It doesn't replace it. A vague prompt from an expert still gets better results than a detailed prompt from someone who doesn't understand the subject.

Principle 2: Context Is Everything

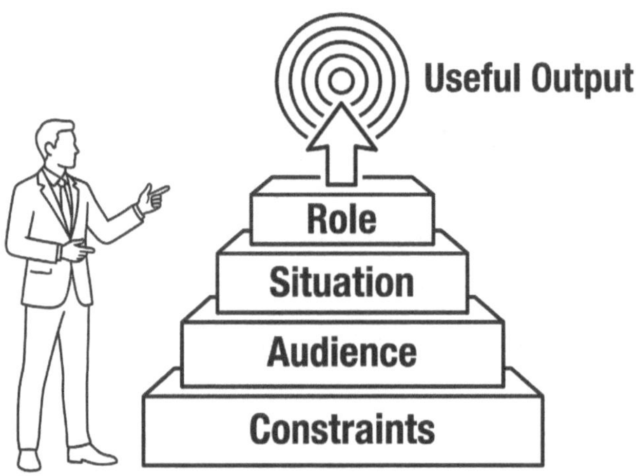

Context narrows the prediction. More context, better output.

This is the single biggest lever for improving your AI results is to **give it what it needs to succeed.**

Remember that definition from the last chapter? AI is a word prediction machine trained on the general internet. Without context, it predicts the most generic, average words possible. With context, it narrows its prediction to your specific situation.

Here's what good context looks like:

- **Role:** Who should the AI be? A marketing strategist? An executive coach? A data analyst? Setting a role shapes the perspective and language of the output.
- **Situation:** What's happening? Are you preparing for a board meeting? Responding to a difficult client? Launching a new product?
- **Audience:** Who will read or use the output? Your boss? Your team? A client? Each audience needs different language, detail, and tone.
- **Constraints:** What are the boundaries? Word count, tone, format, what to avoid?

Same task, without context:

"Write an email about the project delay."

Same task, with context:

"You are a project manager communicating with a client who values transparency. Our website project is delayed two weeks due to a third-party vendor issue. The client is already frustrated about the timeline.

Write a 200-word email that acknowledges the delay honestly, explains the cause without making excuses, and presents a revised timeline with a specific safeguard we've added. Tone: confident and solution-focused, not apologetic."

The second version gives AI everything it needs to produce something you can actually send.

Principle 3: Be Specific About What You Want

Vague inputs produce vague outputs. This isn't a flaw in AI. It's how communication works everywhere.

If you told a new assistant "help me with this document," they'd stare at you blankly. But if you said "proofread this for grammar, check that the tone is professional but warm, and flag any sections that feel too technical for a general audience," they'd know exactly what to do.

AI works the same way.

- **Specify the format:** Do you want bullet points or paragraphs? A table? An email? A script?
- **Specify the length:** "Write a three-paragraph response" is better than "write a response." "Give me five bullet points" is better than "summarize this."

- **Specify the tone:** Professional. Casual. Persuasive. Empathetic. Direct.
- **Specify the structure:** "Start with the conclusion, then provide three supporting points, then end with a recommendation."

The more specific you are, the less editing you'll need to do. And less editing means more time saved, which is the whole point.

Principle 4: Have a Conversation, Not an Interrogation

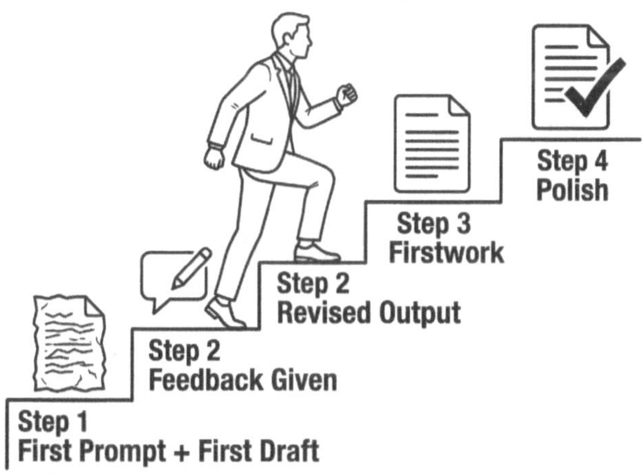

The first response is a draft. The conversation is the work.

Here's where most people get stuck. They type one prompt, get one response, and either use it as-is or give up.

But AI works best through dialogue. The first response is almost never the final answer. It's a starting point.

Think of it this way: if you hired a smart assistant and gave them a task, would you expect perfection on the first attempt? Of course not. You'd review their work, give feedback, and refine together. AI is no different.

After you get an initial response:

- **Ask for adjustments:** "Make this more concise." "Add more detail to the second point." "Change the tone from formal to conversational."

- **Ask for alternatives:** "Give me three different versions of that opening paragraph." "What's another way to frame this argument?"

- **Push back:** "This feels too generic. Can you make it more specific to a healthcare consulting firm?"

Every follow-up you provide makes the next output better. The AI is building on the context of your entire conversation, not just your last message.

Principle 5: Ask for Questions Before Answers

This is my favorite principle, and it's the one that consistently surprises people with how well it works.

Before asking AI to complete a task, try this:

"Before you do this, what questions should you ask me to make sure you get this right?"

What happens next is remarkable. AI will surface the gaps in your request, the information you forgot to include, the assumptions it's making, the decisions that could go either way. It essentially helps you write a better prompt *before* it starts working.

I use this constantly. Whether I'm developing marketing materials, planning a workshop, or writing content, asking AI to interview me first consistently produces better results than jumping straight to the output.

One of my clients, Catherine, a spiritual manifestation coach, experienced this firsthand during a live webinar. I walked through an event planning prompt set that asked AI to surface questions about her coaching business before generating the plan. Questions about the problem she solved, what her methodology looked like, who her ideal client was.

Running through those questions, with Catherine's real business as the input, didn't just produce a better event plan. It opened the eyes of every coach watching that webinar. They could *see* what happened when you gave AI the right context through structured questions before asking it to produce.

Here's the lesson. Let AI ask you questions before it starts working. It's one of the highest-leverage moves you can make.

Principle 6: Trust But Verify

AI can be confidently, convincingly wrong.

It can generate a paragraph that sounds authoritative, includes a specific statistic, attributes a quote to a named researcher, and have every single detail fabricated. Not because it's trying to deceive you. Because it's predicting what *should* come next in a sequence of words, and sometimes what sounds right isn't what's true.

This is called "hallucination," and it's an inherent characteristic of how these systems work. They're not looking things up in a database. They're predicting text. Sometimes those predictions create fiction that reads like fact.

Here's how to handle it:

- **Verify important facts, numbers, names, and claims.** Especially before sharing anything externally.

- **Be extra cautious with specific citations.** AI loves to create plausible-sounding sources that don't exist.

- **Use AI for structure and thinking, not as a fact database.** It's better at organizing your knowledge than at replacing your research.

- **Build verification into your workflow.** Don't treat it as an extra step. Treat it as part of the process.

This isn't a dealbreaker. It's just how the tool works. Once you build in the habit of verification, it becomes second nature, like double-checking your spelling before hitting send.

Principle 7: Make It Your Own

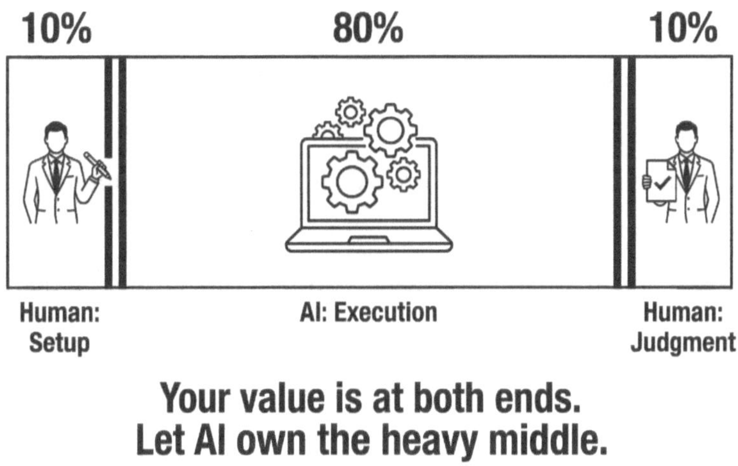

Here's the final principle, and it brings everything full circle. **AI drafts. You finalize.**

Think of your involvement in three parts.

The first 10% is the setup. This is where you specify what you need with precision. The role, the context, the audience, the format, the constraints. The quality of your upfront specification directly determines the quality of what comes out. Don't rush this part.

The middle 80% belongs to AI. Research, first drafts, structure, brainstorming, formatting, multiple versions, and alternatives. The heavy lifting that used to consume your best hours.

The final 10% is your judgment. You review, refine, and add the professional polish that makes the output genuinely yours. Your voice. Your accuracy check. The strategic framing only you can provide.

This is the 10/80/10 rule of AI productivity. Your value shows up at both ends. The precision you bring at the start shapes everything AI produces. The judgment you apply at the end transforms a good draft into excellent work. AI handles the heavy middle, and that's exactly where it excels.

When you maintain this balance, nobody can tell that AI helped produce your work. The finished product reflects your expertise, your perspective, and your standards. AI just helped you get there faster.

One of my students, Rachel, a registered nurse and holistic weight loss coach, demonstrated this perfectly. Rachel learned the prompting principles, and then continued experimenting on her own. She discovered Claude and found it produced writing that better matched her voice. Then she mastered conversational prompting through experimentation.

Rachel used her nursing training to be systematic, evidence-based, and observational skills and applied them . She transferred directly into prompting discipline. She approached AI the way she approached patient care. Gather information, apply a framework, evaluate results, adjust.

The skills that make you good at your profession? They transfer directly into prompting. Rachel's scientific rigor became prompting rigor. Your professional discipline will become yours.

Putting It All Together

Let me walk you through what this looks like in practice.

The task: You need to prepare for a client meeting tomorrow. You need talking points for a status update on their marketing campaign.

Without the 7 Principles:

> *"Give me talking points for a client meeting about their marketing campaign."*

Result: Generic bullet points that could apply to any campaign for any client.

With the 7 Principles:

> *"You are a marketing consultant preparing for a quarterly review meeting with a B2B software company [Role + Context]. The client is detail-oriented and values data over opinions [Audience]. Their content marketing campaign ran for 90 days: organic traffic increased 34%, lead form submissions increased 12%, but email open rates dropped from 24% to 18% [Specifics]. Before creating the talking points,*

> *tell me what additional context would help you create more useful output [Questions first]. The final talking points should be 5-7 bullets, each with the data point and a one-sentence interpretation. Tone: confident and transparent, acknowledge the email issue directly, don't bury it [Format + Constraints]."*

The difference in output quality will astonish you. And once you've written a few prompts like this, the process becomes natural. You'll find yourself automatically including context, specificity, and structure without having to think about it.

Your Action Steps

1. **Take one real task you need to do this week.** Not a hypothetical exercise, an actual deliverable. Write a detailed prompt using all 7 Principles. Compare the output to what you'd get with a quick, vague request.

2. **Have a three-exchange conversation with AI.** Give it a task. Review the output. Give it feedback. Review the revision. Refine one more time. Notice how each exchange improves the result.

3. **Try the "ask me questions first" approach.** On your next task, before AI starts working, ask it what questions it should ask you. Answer them. Then let it work. Notice the difference.

Common mistakes at this stage:

- **Writing prompts like Google searches**, too short, no context, no specificity. AI isn't a search engine. It's a collaborator.
- **Accepting the first response without refinement.** The first response is a draft. Treat it that way.
- **Forgetting to verify factual claims.** Build the verification habit now, before it costs you.

Quick win:

Take a prompt you've used before, anything. Rewrite it with full context, specific instructions, and format requirements. Run both versions and compare. That difference? That's what these principles are worth.

Now you can communicate with AI effectively. You have the A4 Framework from Chapter 4. You have the prompting principles from this chapter. It's time to put both to work. Your first wins are waiting in Chapter 7.

Take the Next Step

Seven principles is a lot to hold in your head at once. The **AI-Powered Professional Foundations Lab** lesson for this chapter is designed to fix that. You'll take a real task from your own work and build a single prompt that uses all seven principles together in one integrated exchange. Not one at a time. All seven, working as a system.

What happens in that exchange is genuinely different from anything you've tried before. You walk away with a polished, real deliverable you built yourself, and a felt sense of what it's like when everything compounds. After this lesson, most people stop thinking about prompting and just start doing it.

Access the lesson at **https://aibizpro.link/aipp-ch-6**

Chapter 7

Your Quick Wins

The Difference Between Knowing and Doing

You understand the AI imperative. You know what AI is. You've learned the prompting principles. You have the A4 Framework. You've confronted the hurdles.

And now comes the moment that separates the professionals who transform from the ones who just read a book.

Action.

Not dramatic, overhaul-your-entire-workflow action. Not "spend the weekend building an AI-powered automation system" action. Small, specific, *this afternoon* action.

Because here's what I've learned from years of teaching AI to professionals. Knowledge without action creates zero change. Understanding the principles is valuable. Applying them is transformative. And the gap between the two is exactly one task.

Let me tell you what closing that gap felt like for me.

The Skill Cascade Effect

One win starts the flywheel. It does not stop.

My early adopters class had a final project. Write a script for a video sales letter. Real business. Real stakes. The class required showing your prompts and outputs publicly.

I'd been practicing for weeks. Some sessions went well, most felt like grinding. But for this final project, something was different. I brought everything together, the context, the specificity, the conversation approach, the iterative refinement.

The AI-generated script was *actually good.*

Not "good for AI." Good, period. Something I could use. Something I would put my name on.

That single win triggered a cascade. I wrote prompts for the webpage. Then the promotional emails. Then elements of the course design. Each success fed the next. Each output proved that the principles worked, which gave me confidence to tackle the next task.

Suddenly, I was off and running.

This is the pattern I've seen over and over: **one meaningful win → confidence → more experimentation → discovery of personal high-value uses.**

It's a flywheel. And the only thing it needs to start spinning is that first win.

That's what this chapter is about. Not theory. Not understanding. Your first wins.

The First Week Quick Win System

FOUR CATEGORIES. ONE PER DAY. REAL RESULTS BY FRIDAY.

I'm going to give you four categories of quick wins. Each one represents a type of task that AI handles exceptionally well. Your job this week is to try one from each category.

Not all four on Monday. One per day. Five days, four categories, plus a repeat day for whatever worked best.

Quick Win Category 1: Communication Tasks

What this covers: Emails, meeting agendas, status updates, memos, the communication work that fills your day.

Why AI excels here: Communication tasks follow patterns. They need specific tones for specific audiences. AI is exceptionally good at generating drafts that match the context you provide.

Your step-by-step:

1. Pick a real email you need to send today

2. Write this prompt:

   "You are a [your role] writing an email to [recipient and their role]. The purpose is [specific purpose]. The tone should be [professional/friendly/direct/diplomatic]. The email should be [length: 2-3 paragraphs / 5 bullet points / etc.]. Key points to include: [list them]. Things to avoid: [anything sensitive or off-limits]."

3. Review the output. Adjust the tone if needed. Add your personal touch.

4. Send it.

What to notice: How long did this take compared to writing from scratch? How much editing did you need to do? How close was the first draft to what you wanted?

Quick Win Category 2: Research and Synthesis

What this covers: Summarizing articles, preparing for meetings, gathering background information, competitive intelligence.

Why AI excels here: Processing and synthesizing large amounts of information is AI's sweet spot. It doesn't get tired, doesn't lose focus, and can organize information in whatever structure you need.

Your step-by-step:

1. Find an article, report, or document you need to read but haven't made time for
2. Paste the key content into your AI tool with this prompt:

   "Summarize this in 5 bullet points, highlighting: the main argument, key evidence, practical implications for a [your role] in [your industry], and anything I should question or verify. Then give me 3 questions this raises that I should consider."

3. Read the summary. Use it to decide if the full document is worth your time.
4. If it is, you now have a framework for reading it efficiently.

If it isn't, you just saved yourself thirty minutes.

What to notice: How much time did this save? Was the summary accurate? Did the AI surface anything you would have missed in a quick skim?

Quick Win Category 3: Document Support

What this covers: Report outlines, first drafts, editing and improvement, reformatting.

Why AI excels here: Structuring information and generating drafts that follow specified formats. AI eliminates the blank-page problem. You're editing and refining instead of creating from nothing.

Your step-by-step:

1. Identify a document you need to create this week, a report, a proposal, a plan

2. Write this prompt:

   "Help me create an outline for a [type of document] about [topic]. The audience is [who will read this]. It should cover: [main points]. The goal is [what the document should accomplish]. Structure it in [format: sections with subsections / numbered steps / executive summary + details]. For each section, include 2-3 bullet points of what should be covered."

3. Review the outline. Reorganize anything that's out of

order. Add missing points.

4. If you want, take the outline back to AI: "Now draft the first section in complete prose. Use a [tone] tone and keep it to approximately [length]."

What to notice: How does starting from an outline change the writing process? Is it faster than starting from scratch?

Quick Win Category 4: Thinking Partner

What this covers: Brainstorming, decision analysis, problem reframing, seeing your work from different perspectives.

Why AI excels here: AI can generate volume and variety of ideas without the constraints of human cognitive biases. It can also help you see blind spots by role-playing different perspectives.

Your step-by-step:

1. Bring a real decision or problem you're working on

2. Write this prompt:

   "I'm a [your role] facing this situation: [describe it clearly]. I'm considering [your current thinking]. Before I decide, help me think through this: (1) What am I not seeing? (2) What could go wrong with my current approach? (3) What would someone who disagrees with me say? (4) What's an alternative approach I haven't considered?"

3. Read the response with an open mind. You won't agree

with everything. That's the point. The value is in the perspectives you hadn't considered.

4. Use whatever's useful. Discard what isn't.

What to notice: Did AI surface anything you genuinely hadn't thought of? How does it feel to have a "devil's advocate" on demand?

This category often surprises people the most. Professionals who expected AI to be useful only for writing tasks discover that AI as a thinking partner is where the real transformation happens. You're not outsourcing your thinking. You're *expanding* it. You're getting perspectives that would normally require scheduling meetings with three different colleagues, each with their own biases and blind spots.

One of my coaching clients put it this way: "It's like having a team of advisors who are always available, never offended by my questions, and never push their own agenda." That's a good description of AI as thinking partner, useful not because it's always right, but because it always has a different angle to offer.

Your First Week Plan

Make this concrete. Block these in your calendar.

- **Monday, Communication:** Draft one email with AI. Time yourself. Compare to your usual speed.

- **Tuesday, Research:** Summarize one article or document.

Evaluate the accuracy. Notice the time saved.

- **Wednesday, Document:** Create an outline for one deliverable. Use it as your starting point.
- **Thursday, Thinking Partner:** Bring one decision to AI. Ask for perspectives you haven't considered.
- **Friday, Best Repeat:** Whichever category felt most valuable, do another one. Build on what's working.

The professionals in my coaching classes who followed this pattern, real tasks, daily practice, building on success, were using AI "daily or weekly" by the end of the program. Those who dabbled without structure plateaued.

Structure beats willpower. Follow the plan.

The Compound Effect

Here's what happens when you complete this first week:

- **Confidence compounds.** Each successful task tells your brain that *this works.* That confidence makes the next task easier. And the next. And the next.
- **Skill compounds.** Each prompt you write teaches you something about how to communicate with AI. By Friday, your prompts will be noticeably better than Monday's, without any additional instruction.

- **Discovery compounds.** As you use AI on different types of tasks, you'll start noticing opportunities you hadn't seen before. "Wait, I could use this for *that* too?" Moments like these are when AI stops being a tool you use sometimes and becomes a collaborator you rely on daily.

- **Time compounds.** If you save thirty minutes on Monday, thirty minutes on Tuesday, and thirty minutes on Wednesday, you've reclaimed an hour and a half by mid-week. That's time for strategic work, creative thinking, or simply leaving the office on time.

The goal isn't to do everything with AI. The goal is to find *your* highest-value uses, the tasks where AI saves you the most time while maintaining or improving quality. Those will be different for every professional. This week helps you discover yours.

For a project manager, the highest-value use might be generating status updates and meeting agendas. For a marketing director, it might be drafting campaign briefs and analyzing competitor messaging. For a consultant, it might be building presentation frameworks and research summaries.

You won't know your highest-value uses until you experiment across categories. That's exactly why the First Week Plan covers all four: communication, research, documents, and thinking partner. By Friday, you'll have data on where AI creates the most value in *your* specific work, not someone else's.

Your Move

I have one request.

Don't put this book down and think, *I'll try this next week.* Or *I'll start Monday.* Or *Let me finish reading a few more things about AI first.*

Do one quick win right now.

Open your AI tool. Pick the easiest one from the four categories above. Spend ten minutes. See what happens.

That's it. Ten minutes. One task.

Not because ten minutes will transform your career. But because the gap between "I know about AI" and "I use AI" is exactly one action wide. Cross it now, and the momentum carries you forward.

Common mistakes to avoid:

- **Starting with high-stakes tasks.** Your first wins should be low-risk. Important enough to be useful, forgiving enough that imperfection doesn't matter.

- **Expecting perfection on first tries.** Your first prompt won't be your best. That's not failure. That's learning.

- **Not tracking what works.** After each quick win, spend thirty seconds noting what worked, what didn't, what you'd do differently. These notes compound into personalized AI wisdom.

Your quick win, right now:

Before you turn to the Closer, complete ONE task from the categories above. Any one. Just start.

You now have everything you need to begin your AI-powered professional journey. The understanding. The principles. The framework. The strategies for when it gets hard. And your first quick wins to build momentum.

What started as an overwhelming technology has become a clear path forward. Let's talk about where that path leads.

Take the Next Step

No template this time. The Chapter 7 lesson in the **AI-Powered Professional Foundations Lab** is where the training wheels come off. You'll pick a real task from your work, write your own prompt from scratch using everything you've learned, work through the conversation, verify the output, and time yourself.

You walk away with a finished deliverable and a clear number showing exactly how much faster AI made you. This is the lesson where most people stop wondering whether they can do this and start knowing they can.

Access the lesson at **https://aibizpro.link/aipp-ch-7**

Chapter 8

Your AI-Powered Future

Remember Where This Started

It was a summer evening in 2022. I was staring at four thousand AI-generated words that were completely useless. Editing them would have taken longer than writing from scratch.

This is not a magic wand, I told myself. *It's going to take some skill and knowledge.*

That was the "before."

Here's the "after." Those same types of tasks now take a fraction of the time. Blog posts, marketing content, email sequences, client deliverables. Not because AI became magic. But because I learned how to communicate with it. I found a framework. I developed the skills.

And now you have those skills too.

What You Now Have

Let me take you through what you've actually accomplished in this book.

Chapter 1: The AI Imperative, You understood why this moment matters. Seventy-five percent of knowledge workers are already using AI. Seventy-one percent of leaders prefer AI-skilled candidates. The gap is widening daily, and you've decided to be on the right side of it.

Chapter 2: The Promise That Didn't Deliver, You recognized that your frustration with AI wasn't personal failure. The hype cycle and the skill gap created a predictable pattern of disappointment. Understanding this freed you to approach AI with realistic expectations and the right framework.

Chapter 3: Demystifying AI, You got the only technical understanding you actually need. AI is a word prediction machine trained on the general internet. Generic input produces generic output. Your domain expertise is the advantage that makes AI genuinely useful.

Chapter 4: The A4 Framework, You have your complete roadmap. Accelerate, Amplify, Augment, Automate, four progressive stages, each building on the last. No more random experimentation. You know exactly where to start and where this leads.

Chapter 5: Overcoming the Hurdles, You confronted the five obstacles that stop most professionals dead in their tracks. "I don't know where to start." "I don't have time to learn." "I'm not technical enough." "I tried it and got bad results." "There are too many tools and constant changes." You learned that every one of these hurdles is psychological, not technical. And you got specific, tested strategies for overcoming each one, not platitudes, but approaches that have worked for real professionals in real situations.

Chapter 6: The Prompting Foundation, You learned the 7 Prompting Principles that turn frustrating interactions into productive ones. Context, specificity, conversation, verification, communication skills, not technical skills. You already had the foundation. Now you know how to apply it.

Chapter 7: Your Quick Wins, You have proven first steps. Communication, research, documents, thinking partner, four categories of immediate wins with step-by-step guides. And a first-week plan to build momentum starting today.

This isn't theory anymore. You have the foundation.

Your Competitive Advantage

Here's what most people don't fully grasp about where you stand now.

The gap between AI-enabled and AI-resistant professionals isn't static. It's accelerating. Every week, AI tools become more capable. The professionals who've built foundational skills, the skills you now have, absorb those advances naturally. They're on an escalator that's getting faster.

The professionals who haven't built those skills? They're standing still while the escalator carries others away.

You're on the escalator now.

When new AI tools emerge, and they will, constantly, you'll evaluate them through your framework. Does this help me Accelerate something? Amplify something? Augment a capability? Automate a workflow? You won't chase every shiny announcement. You'll adopt the tools that genuinely advance your work and ignore the rest.

When career opportunities arise, you'll bring capabilities that differentiate you. Not because you became a technical expert. Because you learned to communicate with AI effectively and apply it systematically to real work.

Where This Leads

This book gave you the foundation. The series takes you to mastery.

Book 2: Accelerate shows you how to systematically speed up your routine work. Advanced prompting architecture, personal prompt libraries, voice calibration, batch processing. What takes hours will take minutes.

Book 3: Amplify teaches you to multiply your impact by elevating the quality and depth of your work. You'll learn to produce outputs that would have required far more time and effort before AI, and then extend the reach of that stronger work into presentations, social content, and more formats that serve different audiences.

Book 4: Augment expands your capabilities. You'll learn to deliver results beyond your current skill level using expert frameworks paired with AI execution.

Book 5: Automate shows you how to build systems that work while you don't. Strategic automation with human oversight where it matters.

Each book goes deep into one stage of the A4 Framework. Together, they create a complete education in professional AI integration, the kind of progressive curriculum that most AI training completely lacks.

But here's what matters most. You don't have to wait for those books to keep growing. Everything in this book is actionable right now. The prompting principles work today. The A4 Framework guides your decisions today. The quick wins build momentum today. The series expands your capabilities over time, but the foundation you've built is already enough to start transforming how you work.

Your Path Forward

Here's what I want you to do:

Today: Complete one Quick Win from Chapter 7. Any one. Just start.

This Week: Follow the First Week Plan:

- Monday: One communication task
- Tuesday: One research task

- Wednesday: One document task
- Thursday: One thinking partner task
- Friday: Repeat what worked best

This Month: Apply the 7 Prompting Principles to every AI interaction. Notice what improves. Track what saves you the most time. Start identifying your personal high-value uses.

By the end of the month, you'll have genuine experience. You'll know what works for you. You'll have momentum that carries forward without effort.

And here's what I've seen happen after that first month. You'll start noticing opportunities everywhere. A meeting that used to require thirty minutes of prep becomes a five-minute AI collaboration. A report that consumed your Friday afternoon gets drafted in an hour on Wednesday. A brainstorming session that used to feel like pulling teeth becomes energizing because you have a thinking partner who never gets tired.

The shift is gradual, then sudden. One day you'll realize you haven't worried about AI overwhelm in weeks. You'll have your preferred tools, your go-to prompting patterns, and a growing sense of what's possible. That's when the real creativity starts. You stop thinking about *how* to use AI and start thinking about *what you could build* with it.

The Gap Will Keep Widening

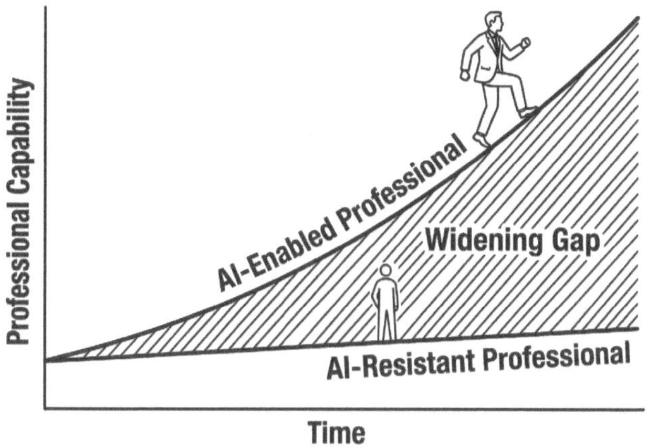

You are on the escalator now. Keep moving.

I want to leave you with a final truth.

The AI transformation of professional work isn't slowing down. It's accelerating. The tools available six months from now will make today's look limited. The professionals who've built foundational skills will absorb those advances naturally.

Some professionals will surf this wave. They'll move from AI-curious to AI-enabled to AI-powered.

Others will resist. Delay. Wait for the "right time" that never comes. And eventually discover that the gap has become very difficult to close.

You've made your choice. You're building the skills, developing the framework, and taking the action that puts you in the first group.

That summer evening in 2022, the one where I stared at four thousand useless words and wondered if AI would ever be useful, feels like a lifetime ago. Not because the technology changed overnight. Because I changed how I approached it.

You're at your own starting line right now. And just like I discovered. This is the worst your AI skills will ever be. Every day forward, you get better. Every month, the tools get better. The compounding starts the moment you take action.

Welcome to your AI-powered professional life.

Remember. This is the worst your AI skills will ever be. The only direction from here is up.

There's one thing I've learned from my own journey, from that summer evening staring at four thousand useless words to now writing this book with AI as my collaborator. It's that professionals who succeed with AI aren't the most technical, the most creative, or the most experienced. They're the ones who started and kept going.

You've already started. By reading this book, by understanding these principles, by committing to action, you've taken the step that most of your colleagues haven't.

Now go make it count. Complete your first Quick Win. Then your second. Then your third.

The rest takes care of itself.

Coming Next in the Series

The foundation is built. The road continues.

Book 2: ACCELERATE

Speed Up Your Existing Work with AI-Powered Efficiency

In this book, you built the foundation, why AI matters, how to communicate with it, and the framework for progressive mastery. Book 2 takes you deep into the first A4 stage, Acceleration.

You'll discover:

The Acceleration Mindset, How to think systematically about speed and identify your highest-leverage acceleration opportunities

Advanced Prompting Architecture, Multi-step prompts, chain prompting, and the five components of high-performance prompts

Your Personal Prompt Library, Building a collection of proven prompts customized to your work

Voice and Style Calibration, Teaching AI to write in your voice, not generic AI-speak

Batch Processing and Speed Optimization, Processing multiple tasks simultaneously for maximum efficiency

By the end of Book 2, the routine tasks that consume your mornings will take minutes. You'll have systems that maintain quality at speeds you didn't think possible.

Your acceleration journey continues...

Take the Next Step

If you've been working through the **AI-Powered Professional Foundations Lab** lessons as you've gone, you're about to finish this book with eight real outputs in your hands. This final lesson pulls everything together. You'll use AI to synthesize everything you've built into a personalized 30-day integration plan. Your top AI-ready tasks. Your A4 progression map. Your primary hurdle and how to move past it. Your biggest win. All of it becomes a week-by-week plan built around your actual work.

This is the bridge between finishing the book and making AI a permanent part of how you work. Go finish it.

Access the course at **https://aibizpro.link/aipp-ch-8**

Acknowledgements

Writing a book about artificial intelligence means standing at a crossroads. The old world valued expertise built in isolation. The new world rewards expertise built in community. This book exists because of the community that formed around me.

Darby Rollins was my entry point into generative AI. As the founder of Gen AI University, Darby did more than teach me the mechanics of prompting. He showed me the fastest path to mastery runs through community. His generosity and freely sharing his knowledge without reservation was a principle I adopted and built the rest of my AI journey upon. Through Darby, I connected with Kelly Tenney, Opher Brayer, and Glenn Dietzel. Three people who each pushed my learning learning past traditional boundaries.

Kelly Tenney gave me the push I needed to move from experimenting to actually building. As the founder of Teach Your Brilliance and a lecturer at California State University, Long Beach, Kelly is the kind of teacher who gets you moving. She pushed me past my initial roadblocks and into real application, and that made all the difference.

Opher Brayer is a true polymath. As Co-Founder and Chief Scientific Officer at Impro.AI and methodology developer at Stages, Opher taught me the value of systems thinking. He has a rare ability to see across disciplines and connect ideas that most people would never put together. Every conversation with Opher makes you smarter.

Glenn Dietzel is a master of developing frameworks for business strategy. As a world-class business consultant and co-founder of multiple AI-focused companies, Glenn showed me how to take complex AI possibilities and turn them into clear, actionable business strategies. He thinks in frameworks, and he taught me to do the same.

Rich Schefren changed how I think about AI as a tool for personal and professional development. Through his ZenithMind Program, Rich helped me understand how AI can be calibrated to the way I actually think, based on my personality and working style. Through ZenithPro, he showed me how to build and run a business with AI at its core. Rich is one of the sharpest strategic minds I have come across.

Mark Kashef is the person I turn to when I need to stay current on what AI is actually doing right now. Through his Early AI-dopters community and YouTube channel, Mark delivers up-to-date technical knowledge in a way that anyone can absorb and apply. He is prolific, consistent, and generous with his knowledge.

The Growth Collective is a unique group of entrepreneurs. They bring decades of combined experience, a willingness to share, and a genuine desire to help that is rare among busy people with full lives and serious businesses. Shelly Berman, Steve Cary, Kevin Kuykendall, John Munsell, Taireez Niswander, Omar Paloma, Keyan Razi, and Robin Yearsley each brought a perspective that sharpened my thinking in ways I am still discovering.

Chantal Cox and Guin White are excellent coaches, visionaries, and savvy AI entrepreneurs. Building the AI Biz Connection the AI Coach Connection Community alongside them has been one of the most rewarding parts of this journey. They bring complementary strengths that make the work better, and they push me to think bigger about what is possible.

These professional relationships shaped the ideas in this book. But my family shaped me.

I am blessed beyond measure with four amazing children who remind me every day why this work matters. Each are well-rounded high achievers with unshakeable moral character. They make me proud every day and inspire me to keep learning, creating, and sharing.

And to my wife, Jodi. For every hour I spent building, you were there. You never once complained. You told me how valuable this work was, encouraged me to share it with the people who need it most, and pushed me to keep pursuing this dream. Your support has never wavered. That belief is woven into every page of this book.

This would not exist without any of you.

About the Author

Every business professional carries a version of the same frustration. There is more you could accomplish. More impact you could have. More ways your career could advance. But the hours that low-value tasks drain from your day are hours you never get back, and the high-value work keeps waiting.

Bruce Fleck, PhD, MBA, knows that feeling firsthand. What makes his story different is what he chose to do about it. Years before ChatGPT made AI something everyone wanted to try, he was already working through early, expensive, and imperfect tools, determined to find a better way. The frustration wasn't unique. The choice to solve it early was.

Through early experiments with automated writing software and first-generation AI platforms, he discovered what most professionals still struggle to see. AI is more than a productivity tool. It fundamentally changes what one person can accomplish. The question stops being how much can I get done and starts being what will have the most impact.

That discovery, combined with over 30 years of corporate management experience, a PhD in Psychology specializing in technology adoption, and an MBA in Marketing, led him to develop the A4

AI Integration Framework (Accelerate, Amplify, Augment, Automate). His framework gives non-technical professionals a clear path from frustrated beginner to confident AI collaborator. Unlike prompt collections or tool-specific tutorials, it teaches thinking principles that work across every AI platform and use case.

Having coached dozens of professionals through this transformation, Bruce has seen firsthand what the right guidance does. Overwhelm becomes capability. Confusion becomes confidence. He is the co-founder of The AI Biz Connection and founder of A IBizProfessional.com. One conviction guides everything he does. Technology should empower people, not confuse them, control them, or replace them.

Bruce knows because he made that transition himself, the hard way, before there were roadmaps. This book is the one he wishes he had.

Connect with Bruce at BruceFleck.com and AIBizProfesssional.c om.

Made in United States
Troutdale, OR
06/07/2026

49767669R10070